Child-care and the psychology of development

Feminists have long argued for the provision of day-care facilities so that mothers may be free to work outside the house. The call has enjoyed little support from politicians and experts, however. Feminists have been seen to stand for women's interests, and psychologists and pedagogues for children's – as if the two were opposed. Only recently have the opinions of politicians and experts begun to change. Yet, even so, a positive policy on day-care and the production of pedagogical and psychological knowledge of the consequences for children and parents is still lacking.

Elly Singer aims to analyse the historical roots of the contradictions, dilemmas and vicissitudes of power in the current political debates on child-care inside and outside the home. The history of development psychology is traced against the background of international social movements to reform child-care, especially in England, the USA and the Netherlands. What are their common grounds? Elly Singer's book challenges familiar concepts and opens up new ways of thinking to meet the new situations in which many children and parents live.

Elly Singer is a researcher and lecturer at the Universities of Utrecht and Amsterdam. She has experience in education and child-care and has undertaken numerous studies on the psychology of parenthood, child-rearing practices and provision, and professional intervention in problem situations. She has been an advisor to the OECD, the European Community and various national research and policy organisations in the Netherlands.

Critical Psychology
Series editors

John Broughton
Columbia University
David Ingleby
Vakgroep Ontwikkeling en Socialisatie, Utrecht
Valerie Walkerdine
Birmingham Polytechnic

Since the 1960s there has been widespread disaffection with traditional approaches in psychology, and talk of a 'crisis' has been endemic. At the same time, psychology has encountered influential contemporary movements such as feminism, neo-marxism, post-structuralism, and post-modernism. In this climate, various forms of 'critical psychology' have developed vigorously.

Unfortunately, such work – drawing as it does on unfamiliar intellectual traditions – is often difficult to assimilate. The aim of the Critical Psychology series is to make this exciting new body of work readily accessible to students and teachers of psychology, as well as presenting the more psychological aspects of this work to a wider social scientific audience. Specially commissioned works from leading critical writers will demonstrate the relevance of their new approaches to a wide range of current social issues.

Titles in the series include

The crisis in modern social psychology
And how to end it
Ian Parker

The psychology of the female body
Jane M. Ussher

Significant differences
Feminism in psychology
Corinne Squire

The mastery of reason
Cognitive development and the production of rationality
Valerie Walkerdine

Child-care and the psychology of development

Elly Singer

Translated by Ann Porcelijn

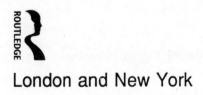

London and New York

First published 1992
by Routledge
11 New Fetter Lane, London EC4P 4EE

Simultaneously published in the USA and Canada
by Routledge
a division of Routledge, Chapman and Hall, Inc.
29 West 35th Street, New York, NY 10001

© 1992 Elly Singer

Typeset in Palatino by LaserScript Limited, Mitcham, Surrey
Printed and bound in Great Britain by
Mackays of Chatham PLC, Chatham, Kent

British Library Cataloguing in Publication Data
Singer, Elly *1948*–
    Child-care and the psychology of development. – (Critical
    psychology).
    1. Children. Day care
    I. Title II. Series
    362.712

Library of Congress Cataloging-in-Publication Data
Singer, Elly, 1948–
    [Kinderopvang en de moeder-kindrelatie. English]
    Child care and the psychology of development/Elly Singer;
    translated by Ann Porcelijn.
    p. cm. – (Critical psychology series)
    Translation of: Kinderopvang en de moeder-kindrelatie.
    Includes bibliographical references and index.
    1. Child care – History. 2. Child care services – History.
    3. Child development – History. I. Title. II. Series: Critical psychology.
    HQ778.5.S56 1992
    649′.1 – dc20   91-3320
                                                                  CIP

ISBN 0–415–05591–1
       0–415–05592–X (pbk)

The translation of this book was co-financed by the Kohnstamm
Foundation.

Contents

Chapter 1

Women and children

The provision of child-care facilities is extremely controversial. It is an area in which the two-sided attitudes towards women and children can become bitter.

At the end of the sixties, mothers who wanted to work outside the home took action to demand good and affordable child-care facilities. Both politicians and experts reacted with shock. Daily separations from the mother were supposed to be very damaging to the child; the child was not to be sacrificed to the mother.

Nowadays, the moral indignation towards mothers working outside the home has died down, but the undertone of condemnation still remains. While even more mothers now work outside the home without good child-care facilities, the prevailing attitude is still one of hesitation and restraint. Where is the sense of responsibility which is necessary for mothers to be able to entrust part of the child-care to others?

In the discussion on child-care facilities, the child's 'best interests' are very often placed opposite the mother's, as though the interests of children are quite irreconcilable with the interests of their mothers; as though fathers and other adults have no responsibility to care for children. What has made us think like this? This question has led me on a search through history, to find the background to these ways of thinking about mothers and children.

THE 'ANTI-CHILD-CARE FACILITIES' ATTITUDE IN WESTERN COUNTRIES.

I started my research in the Netherlands, but soon realized that the provision of child-care facilities is still a controversial issue in other Western, industrialized countries. With the exception of the Scandinavian countries, all West European countries suffer, to some extent, from a lack of arrangements, support and facilities for the care of the children of working mothers (Phillips and Moss, 1988). The possibilities for taking leave of absence are far too restricted for mothers and fathers; there is a lack of part-time jobs, or jobs with flexible working hours; fathers play a relatively small part in the daily care of children; there is a lack of good and affordable child-care facilities; workers in child-care are underpaid. In the United States the situation was apparently not much better (Kamerman and Kahn, 1981; Phillips, 1990).

Generally speaking, therefore, the arrangements for the children of mothers working outside the home are inadequate. Compared to other West European countries, the Netherlands, along with England and Ireland, are the countries which have made the fewest arrangements, and have the lowest percentage of working mothers. This is apparent from an international study carried out in EEC countries in 1987 (Phillips and Moss, 1988). For instance, in Denmark, a country with an extensive system of child-care facilities subsidized by the government, more than 70 per cent of mothers with children under the age of 5, work for thirty or more hours a week outside the home. In France and Belgium, where there are fewer facilities than Denmark but more than in the Netherlands and England, approximately 50 per cent of mothers work outside the home. In the Netherlands, Ireland and England, less than 30 per cent of mothers work outside the home; many of these mothers work only nineteen hours a week or less. In these countries, policies as well as work participation are determined by woman's caring role within the family.

However, policies and women's work participation do not necessarily have to be so clearly connected. For instance, in the United States in 1987, nearly 60 per cent of the mothers with children under the age of 6 were working outside the home, many of them full-time, while the policy of the authorities at central and local level were extremely reserved (Phillips, 1990). The child-care facilities there are nearly all in the hands of private enterprise. These take the form of profit-making centres. Family day-care, private arrangements for care-taking at home, and care-takers for the family are also used. Child-care in the United States has barely any status, a fact made apparent in the underpayment of the teachers and care-takers. An extremely large staff turn-over, a lack of trained staff and poor quality child-care facilities also confirm the low status accorded to workers in this field. Attitudes remain restricted to the ideal of the mother at home, or parents who take care of the daily needs of their children themselves. In practice, reality is different for the majority of families. The lack of arrangements and facilities for children and working mothers points not only to discrimination against women working outside the home, but also to the undervaluation of the caring task that mothers have traditionally fulfilled at home: in financial terms, caring for children is hardly worthwhile!

Consequently, in all the Western industrialized countries, with the exception of Scandinavia, there is an affinity between the policies towards mothers working outside the home. At a scientific level there also seem to be affinities in thought on child-care outside the home. The present Dutch child studies are strongly orientated to research which is being done in the United States and England. Bowlby's and Ainsworth's attachment theory are extremely influential. This theory causes child-care outside the home to be regarded with suspicion: child-care outside the home is supposedly a risk-factor (Belsky, 1988). Other researchers try to approach study of child-care facilities with a more positive attitude. How does it work, and what can or needs to be done better (Clarke-Stewart, 1989; Phillips, 1990)? In the Anglo-Saxon research world, the discussion is raised again and again on whether child-care outside the home is bad, and the advocates and opponents repeatedly cross swords.

RECONSIDERATION

Meanwhile, the number of working mothers is growing fast. In 1970, 29 per cent of mothers with children under the age of 6 were working in the United States; in 1980 this percentage had risen to 43 per cent; in 1990 to 58 per cent; and in 1995 two-thirds of all pre-school-age children will have a mother in the work force (Phillips, 1990). In the Netherlands the number of mothers working is much smaller, but it is growing. In the Netherlands the percentage of working mothers with children up to the age of 4 rose from 9 per cent in 1971, to 15.6 per cent in 1979 and 24.8 per cent in 1985. In 1995 it is expected that 30 per cent of mothers with pre-school children will be working outside the home (Singer, 1989; Phillips and Moss, 1988).

In spite of the conservative policy and the experts' warnings, the number of child-care facilities is also growing rapidly, even though in the United States, England and the Netherlands, most children are cared for by family, care-taker at home or child-minders. The numbers of child-care centres and organized guest-parent care groups are also growing. In 1969 there were sixty-five day-care centres in the Netherlands, mainly for families with financial or socio-medical problems. In 1975 there were 162 day-care centres also being used by mothers wanting to work outside the home; in 1984 the number had risen to 240; and in 1989 there were 635. At a rough estimate only about 1 per cent of all 0–4-year-olds attend a day-care centre, but this percentage is a great deal higher in the city areas where industry also organizes child-care centres for its employees. It is apparent from the United States that an explosive growth of child day-care centres is possible. There, in 1965 between 2 and 6 per cent of children under the age of 3 years attended a day-care centre, while at the present time more than 20 per cent of this age group are now attending a day-care centre. Between 1982 and 1985 the percentage of children under 1 year of age, and in day-care centres, grew from 8 to 18 per cent (Phillips, 1990).

In countries like the Netherlands, the United States and Britain, with a conservative child-care policy, systematic data on the quality of care is lacking. There is also no control, or hardly any, on the quality of this care. Now and then scandalous stories come to light: of British child minders with far too many children, with no outdoor play area, who care minimally for the children and just try to keep them quiet (Mayall and Petrie, 1977; Jackson and Jackson, 1979): of Dutch child-care centres that have not even been checked for basic fire safety (FNV, 1989); and of American day-care centres where the staff work for less than a year, and children are continually being confronted with changing teachers and groups (Whitebook, Howes and Phillips, 1990).

How long can child-care experts and politicians permit themselves to ignore what is going on within child-care facilities? How long will we continue the discussion about the (supposedly) damaging effects of child-care outside the home on young children's development, without doing our utmost to improve the situation for children and working parents?

If, in the future, large groups of children are going to spend three to five days a week outside the family from a very young age, it can only mean a great change in the familiar pattern of upbringing. New traditions of upbringing are never developed without difficulties and risks which have to be appreciated. Child-care outside the home can bring an ideal of upbringing closer, but it can also cause a great deal of misery, if fast and cheap expansion is sought at the cost of quality.

The wish to clear the way for developmental-psychological discussions with an eye to the problems of child-care facilities, without idealizing the 'at home with mother' situation, has made me reconsider the current developmental-psychological theories about mothers, children and child-care outside the home. I wanted to know why thinking in opposites was so strong; why policy makers, as well as pedagogues and developmental psychologists, all use the terms 'child-orientated' and 'mother orientated' as though the interests of working mothers and children are totally opposed. I also wanted to study to what extent the current theories of early child development can be used in empirical research into the development of children who, from early babyhood, have been cared for outside the home for part of the day. Many developmental psychologists had been extremely negative about care outside the home for very young children, and this attitude could be related to the basic concepts of their theories. To what extent are the elements of family upbringing and child-care facilities that are taken for granted, included at policy level, in developmental psychological terms and research? To what extent are we imprisoned in categories of thought from the past, making it impossible for us to ask the questions needed in a (future) situation where many children, from birth, are going to spend a large part of their day outside the home?

THE CHILD AS A 'CULTURAL INVENTION'

The reconsideration of the philosophies on children and mother-hood that I had in mind corresponded to a broader tendency towards a more critical reflection on the subject within develop-mental psychology. During the past decade various studies have appeared, questioning the status of scientific knowledge about children in our society. For instance, John and Elizabeth Newson, (1974), pointed to the curious fact that there is no other culture which produces and consumes so much knowledge about children, but, at the same time, that there is no other culture with so much uncertainty amongst its parents/mothers. 'The cult of child psychology' is, according to them, a uniquely Western phenomenon. Feminist researchers have shown how popularized scientific knowledge is brought into the home through women's magazines, in order to tell mothers about the complexity of their children's inner life, and how it is the mother's fault if their children get into difficulties and have too many problems (Ehrenreich and English, 1979; Riley, 1983). Others, like Christopher Lasch (1977), were not so concerned about the mothers' difficult position, but more about the undermining of parental/fatherly authority by the army of experts armed with scientific knowledge marching into the private family environment. Micha de Winter (1986) analysed the dream of the predictable child, fed by a science that promises the controllability of life.

In 'The American child and other cultural inventions' (1983), William Kessen defends the statement that the child, as well as the developmental psychologist, are both cultural inventions. Both have to be understood as parts of a broader culture, and both are influenced by 'greater powers' within the culture. Changes in Western culture which have significantly altered the lives of and the thought on children are: industrialization, the separation of paid work outside the home from the family, the separation of the men's world from the women's world, and the creation of class differences. A separate world was created where children were allowed to play, learn and spend their free time, first in the upper and middle classes, who were able to afford a nursery, nanny or mother at home. Poor children were herded together in national schools.

According to Kessen, developmental psychology is one of the creative powers behind the new images of children. As a science, it fed the idea that people could be 'made' through the application of scientific knowledge to the practice of child rearing. Developmental psychology gave parents information about their children through magazines and institutions for help and advice on child rearing; they gave schools and therapeutic institutions the instruments with which to measure intelligence and development, and diagnose problems. Various developmental psychologists invented various types of children. As an example of this Kessen mentioned Darwin, who observed his son Doddy and discovered 'emotions'; Baldwin looked at his daughter Polly and discovered 'thought'; Freud observed Anna and saw 'fulfilment of desire'; Watson found 'unconditioned responses' in his son Billy, and Piaget found 'adaptive assimilation' in his daughter Jacqueline. In practice, these scientific terms have become images of how children are, overshadowing the other experiences of parents, teachers and the children themselves. According to Kessen, developmental psychology has developed from a Western culture where children are seen as a separate category, and thus given their own space. In turn, developmental psychology influences the way children are treated in our culture. For this reason Kessen advocates a historical-cultural developmental psychology.

In 'Development in social context' (1986), David Ingleby surveys critical streams within developmental psychology, which have developed independently in the United States and England. He attempted not only to describe human development in an historical context within these streams, but at the same time to explain the origin of developmental psychology as a science, and in its influence on the images of children, child rearing and manners. For the American discussion, the Houston Symposium held in 1981 on 'The Child and Other Cultural Inventions' is, amongst others, of importance. Milestones in the English discussion were *The Integration of a Child into a Social World* (1974), the follow-up to this, *Children of Social Worlds* (1986), and *Changing the Subject* (1984).

All these streams have in common the fact that their roots can be found in criticism of the positivist view of science, current within Anglo-Saxon orientated developmental psychology. In the first place there is criticism of the assumption of the existence of universal laws at work 'in' the child, separate from the social context in which it lives. In discussions about child-care outside the home, we come across this assumption in advocates as well as opponents, who make statements about 'the influence' of the child-care centre on 'the development' of 'the child'. 'The child' could manage quite well without its mother during the day; 'the child' would be damaged by daily separations – as though all children experience child-care centres in the same fashion, or as though all mothers are the same!

A second critical point has a bearing on what is called the

'technological Utopia'. Scientific knowledge of universal laws of development is supposedly applicable to the improvement of the practice of child rearing. Scientific knowledge is supposedly superior to people's wisdom or 'laymen's' knowledge. This supposition implies the conviction that non-scientists, particularly parents and teachers, need expert scientific guidance. 'Real' knowledge must replace superstition; in this way, scientifically descriptive statements become normative statements on how things should be done. But just how 'true' and how 'rational' is our present-day scientific knowledge of children?

A third criticism concerns the values and standards that implicitly play a role in the production of knowledge. Contrary to the self-image of rationality, theories include all sorts of prejudices against the socially lower classes and ethnic minorities. In women's studies the prejudices against women and men and particularly against mothers have been pointed out.

A final criticism concerns the lack of an historical awareness of the social meaning of scientific knowledge within the exercise of the science of positivism. It is wrongly assumed that developmental psychology only describes and explains the development of children/adults. However, science has a great influence on people's lives, because of the manner in which their development is conceptualized (Freud's fulfilment of desire; Watson's conditioned reflexes), the production of techniques for gaining knowledge (tests, observation schedules and so on) and the production of techniques for interventions in mental functioning (for instance, conditioning techniques or techniques on group dynamics). This influence is often transmitted by scientifically schooled experts on child rearing, who give help and advice to parents and teachers. Developmental psychology not only registers, it also collaborates in the 'invention of children'.

Within the streams mentioned by Ingleby (1986), the criticism of developmental psychology orientated to positivism is, to a large degree, unanimous. But their unanimity ends here. There are great differences between the critical streams such as historical materialism, feminism and post-structuralism. A discussion on these streams does not belong within the framework of this study; instead I will restrict myself to the discussion of the theoretical framework which has directed my study.

SOCIAL MOVEMENTS AND DEVELOPMENTAL PSYCHOLOGY

In this study I aimed, in the first place, at shedding some light on the phenomenon of mothers and children being used against each other in discussions about child-care outside the home. The discussions all tend to start from the viewpoint that 'mother-orientated' interests in activities outside the home are basically irreconcilable with 'child-orientated' interests in a safe base at home. In order to do this, I had to find a way of gaining some insight into the historical origins of the terms 'mother's interest' and 'child's interest'.

Following the above-mentioned streams in developmental psychology, my starting point was that within developmental psychological theories, as well as the phenomena to which they are related (children, parents, child-care facilities), are cultural phenomena influenced by a broader cultural-historical context. Processes of change in this broader cultural context, such as industrialization, technological progress and the separation of work and the home, all influence the scientific industry. However, they in no way determine directly the contents of theories and research, but should be seen rather as conditions in which certain problems become apparent. These problems can be analysed in different ways using different scientific theories.

This very general description gives further research very little to go on. In order to give more direction to the research, I have developed working hypotheses on the relations between social movements for child-care facilities, and scientific research into child-care outside the home.

The history of child-care facilities in the Netherlands, Germany, Britain and the United States shows that child-care facilities have been invented several times, or discovered as an instrument for solving social problems. In addition, it is clear that the great streams of thought and innovation in this field were *international movements*. At the start of the nineteenth century there was an infant-school movement for children from the 'poorer classes'. In the second half of the nineteenth century there was a Froebel or kindergarten movement, educating children according to 'their nature'. In the twenties there was the 'nursery-school' movement to make child rearing more scientific. During the sixties and seventies there was a movement for child-care centres in order to break the cycle of poverty at a crucial time in children's lives and provide compensatory education. During the seventies and eighties there was a feminist movement demanding child-care outside the home to make it possible for mothers to work outside the home.

Within these social movements, child-care facilities were seen as an instrument for achieving socio-political aims. By this I mean aims which overreach the upbringing itself, and are related to broader social questions, such as crime prevention, elevation of mankind, emancipation of women and unemployment prevention. Child rearing and child-care facilities were seen as a way of achieving broader social aims.

Theories on mothers/parents and children's development, amongst other things, were used to justify the various aims. In other words, at the social movement level, a natural link was made between social values, standards and aims on the one hand, and scientific theories and research on the other.

The terms 'mother's interest' and 'child's interest' appeared to have a long history within the social movement for child-care facilities. By studying these social movements the normative context of scientific theories could be explained, and the values embodied in scientific concepts; theories and research questions could be discovered.

By taking the social movements as a starting point, I followed the line of earlier studies on the history of developmental psychology, such as that of Siegel and White (1982). They showed, for instance, how the first child studies in the United States were part of a broad social movement in the field of child rearing and education. Round about the turn of the century, new laws and institutions were established to intervene in (family) upbringing. Examples of this are the clinics for babies; homes for mentally and/or physically handicapped children; homes for neglected or criminal children; and the introduction of compulsory schooling.

These new laws and institutions created all sorts of new questions about the knowledge of children. The first developmental psychologists pandered to this need for knowledge. The importance of research into children was often defended, particularly with regard to sponsors, by pointing out its utility in practice. Psychologists can fulfil a useful role as 'problem solvers' within social movements.

In their study, Siegel and White (1982) pointed out that children within these new institutions were being isolated from the rest of society. You could say that special 'children's spaces' developed, making it difficult for children to grow naturally into the adult world. These 'spaces' were socially 'empty', and had to be filled with 'pedagogic action'. Pedagogic action became a mode of behaviour with children which was separate from the action/work of adults. Not only schools, but also infant schools, nursery schools, play groups and day-care centres are all pre-eminently children's spaces. We may therefore assume that experts have played a large part in designing and inventing child-centred methods, manners of working and material in order to fill these socially 'empty' spaces.

The above-mentioned insights can be summarized in the following working hypotheses:

> social movements for child-care facilities form the bridge between the socio-political aims of child centres, and the scientific philosophy about child rearing and early child development;
>
> Science has a partly legitimizing function, partly a problem-solving function, partly an innovative and creative function, particularly in filling the 'empty' spaces created by children being put into 'children's spaces' separate from the world of adults.

The above does not mean that I assume that the social movements and scientific work completely coincide with each other. Scientific production forms a relatively autonomous area with its own logic, internal dynamics, status hierarchy and institutional position in society. Throughout history there have been many examples of great philosophers who were only valued fifty or a hundred years later. Think of the work done by Piaget, which was already known in the thirties in the United States, later forgotten, but rediscovered during the sixties as one of the most important theories of this century. The time has to be ripe. Science is, therefore, relatively autonomous, but the success of a theory depends on the extent to which the central concepts and problem definitions converge with the concepts and problem definitions that exist in the dominant groups of society. A flourishing research practice can develop if the sponsors, the interested parties and scientists all agree on the central concepts in which the problem should be posed.

Before I expand on my research questions, I will first explain what this study is *not*, by using a few recent studies on the history of developmental psychology. In the first place this study is not meant to give a historical summary of influential theories in developmental psychology, something that has already been done by Cairns (1983), for instance; this was based on work carried out by important founders of this profession like Hall, Binet, Freud, Watson, Baldwin and Piaget. In Cairns's study the great philosophers seem to appear in a purely theoretical position. The continuous thread through his study is the idea of scientific progress: by means of additions, byways, dead-ends and break-throughs, the young profession develops itself to adulthood. Practical problems seem to be seen only in terms of slowing down or speeding up this process. The practice is seen as an area in which scientific knowledge can be applied. The latter forms the point of departure for *Science and Patterns of Child Care* (1978), by Elisabeth Lomax. In this book, Lomax gives a summary of theories and their influence on the practice of child rearing. In my study I question not only the presupposition about scientific progress, but also science's innovating influence on the practice.

This study is also not a search for the historical origins of false truths which are a direct result of the power relations of group interests placed outside science in society. In ideological criticism of the seventies, for instance, a direct link was laid between IQ tests in which children from the lower classes scored badly, and capitalistic interests in selecting and concealing class differences (Bowles and Gintis, 1976). In research amongst day-care children into damaging effects of daily separation from the mother, one can see the hand of patriarchy. It is assumed that external scientific interests or factors can influence the contents of scientific work. In this study I do not assume that there is a direct influence. The scientific industry is relatively autonomous. In my study I want to research how, through the level of social movements, relations develop between socio-political aims/interests and scientific theories and research. A second difference from the ideological studies of the seventies is that I am not concerned with unmasking 'false truths', but rather in analysing the 'production of truths'. How does science collaborate in the origination of forms of life for children and parents through conceptualization and observation and measuring instruments, and so on?

Finally, this study is not intended to design a new theory of developmental psychology about mothers, children and child-care outside the home. I am more concerned with the choices made by scientists, who, through their concepts, extract certain characteristics from reality and separate them. This is where the potential power of science lies. What is revealed and what is concealed? What experiences are clarified, and what disappears into obscurity? What values and standards (implicitly) form the basis of this? I hope that, by breaking through certain concepts, space will develop for other experiences that can perhaps offer a link to theories more suited to the changed living conditions of women and children.

THE RESEARCH QUESTIONS

Child-care facilities in this study are seen in a broad context, as every form of part-time care or upbringing of young children outside the family. These facilities were and are given various titles. For instance, in the nineteenth century in the Netherlands there were little children's schools, women's schools, play schools, dame schools, preparatory schools, infant schools, Froebel schools and kindergartens. I have used the English translation of the names, although these are difficult to translate without leading to the wrong associations. The numerous English terms for institutions for young children often indicate realities which can differ from country to country. The abundance of terms reflects the lack of uniformity and clear definitions for the various forms of child-care to which we have become accustomed in our bureaucracy, with its fixed subsidy rules and regulations. In earlier years, the age groups for which the child-care facilities were intended were also never exactly clarified. Nowadays we tend to think in terms of age categories, such as 'the baby' and 'the toddler', but in older texts 'small children' can mean all children under elementary school age.

In the Netherlands, Britain and the United States, in spite of the variety of names, a sharp distinction is often made between 'educative' facilities for young children, 'welfare' facilities and 'care' facilities. The concept of 'child-care facilities' brings these different forms of part-time institutions for young children together under one common denominator. I have done this in order to avoid getting involved with the dividing line which exists between the various facilities. Hidden behind the self-evident distinction between 'educative' and 'care', are worlds of values, standards and images of what is good for mothers and good for children.

The following questions played a central part in my study of the social movements for child-care facilities, and the scientific theories pertaining to them:

1 What socio-political motives formed the basis of social movements for child-care facilities? And, for which categories of children, parents and/or activities were the facilities intended?
2 On the grounds of which pedagogical and psychological theories were certain categories of children, parents and activities determined and found suitable for child-care facilities?
3 What values and (hierarchical) positions in society, at policy and scientific level, were secured and/or affected by including or excluding groups of children from the child-care facilities?
4 Why are the activities of mothers/child rearers outside the upbringing/care of the children, held to be (potentially) damaging to the interests of the children?

As already mentioned, the emphasis in this study is on the large international movement in philosophy and organization of the upbringing of young children outside the home in child-care facilities. An analysis will be given of the socio-political motives, and pedagogical or developmental psychological arguments, as voiced by advocates of certain forms of child-care in the countries from which the movement originated. Following this, I will sketch the way in which these movements gained form in the Netherlands, and in Britain and the United States inasmuch as this is relevant for an insight into the social context of the Anglo-Saxon (-orientated) developmental psychological research into child-care facilities. However, this method does mean that historical specifics of a certain country or area will remain under-exposed.

Finally, I will outline the form of the book. I start with a tale about the first infant school at the end of the eighteenth century. This tale introduces three themes, continually repeated during the history of child-care facilities: social innovation through interventions in family upbringing; the importance of the first years of childhood; and the (ambiguous) position of women. The rest of Chapter 2 is concerned with the socio-political motives behind the infant school movement at the start of the nineteenth century; family upbringing became the standard because it set out and centralized two aims: education and family replacement for the children from 'bad' families. In Chapter 3 enlightened pedagogical theories are discussed. Was the distinction between upbringing (family) and education (school) supported by these pedagogical theories? And, how are theories about upbringing and the development of young children related at a theoretical level to characteristics of the circumstances of upbringing: for instance, in a one-to-one-relationship or in a group situation?

In Chapter 4 women play the main role in the Froebel or kindergarten movement at the end of the nineteenth century. Froebelians combined their feminist demands with a struggle for recognition of motherhood and a more liberal approach to children. Pedagogy should become the women's science. At first glance it would appear that their interests were in direct opposition to those of present-day feminists. What were their socio-political motives, and what theories about mothers and children did they espouse?

Chapter 5 is concerned mainly with the United States at about the turn of the century. The rise of the present-day developmental psychology is placed against a background of new practices in child raising in which there was a need for more information about how children 'really' were. Scientists saw the child centres and nursery schools as an important instrument for 'raising the standard' of upbringing. In nursery schools young children were made visible and researchable for researchers; experiments on the application of scientific knowledge in upbringing could be carried out; through contact with parents, the scientific knowledge could be transmitted to mothers at home. Essentially, all mothers were in need of scientific guidance – according to scientists of the time.

In Chapter 6 we arrive at the period after the Second World War. Some psychologists discovered maternal love as the decisive influence on the development of young children. 'Maternal deprivation' was said to lead to delinquency and psychological disorders. Seen from this point of view, child centres were a danger to public mental health.

However, during the sixties child centres were once again discovered as an instrument for a scientifically justified upbringing. Children from the lower social classes were said to be 'culturally deprived' and their mothers ignorant with regard to upbringing. Through expert encouragement in child centres the children's developmental retardation could be compensated.

However, in the same period child-care centres for the children of working mothers remained extremely controversial. The child needed a sensitive and available mother in order to be able to develop a safe bond with her. Chapter 8 concerns this subject: the attachment theory and the feminist struggle for child-care outside the home.

In the final chapter the questions posed in this study are answered on the basis of the collected material, and conclusions are drawn about the way women and children are defined with respect to each other, within scientific philosophy on the development and upbringing of young children.

Chapter 2

'Suffer the little children to come unto me . . .'

The infant school movement during the first half of the nineteenth century

For the lower classes the infant schools appear like guardian angels of innocence, like caring mothers.

(R.G. Rijkens, 1845)

A TALE

Cast your mind back, if you will, seventy years or more, to a time when man is beginning to work more directly on human civilization . . . . In this period at least, one can come across a real Christian in the Vosges mountains in the Stone valley (. . . . His name is Jan Frederik Oberlin, a 'man who has achieved an immortal name by forming and educating an almost wild people'.

(Berdenis van Berlekom, 1842)

These words represent the beginning of the oldest historical records of Dutch infant school education, and date from 1842. As far as contents and tone are concerned, the story which follows these words can be condensed to the following.

Oberlin had discovered a wretched situation in the Stone valley: no civilization, no welfare, and an ignorant, poverty-stricken community. The school was nothing more than a barn, where children occupied themselves romping about noisily.

Oberlin started building roads and bridges but realized that more was needed. One day, in one of the houses he came across a girl who was seated at her spinning wheel surrounded by children. She sang songs and kept the children amused whilst also teaching them. This was a revelation to Oberlin. His work as an educator of mankind must start with the youngest. Through the children he would reach the parents' hearts, making them receptive to the blessings of civilization and religion. He employed the girl and furnished a spacious room, and thus, in 1770, the first infant school was founded.

The youngest children were allowed to play, and Oberlin taught them to talk. He acknowledged the educative value of spontaneous activity. The older children learned to knit, sew and tend a garden. The school left the mothers free to work on the land and do the housekeeping, and at the same time through the school they learned how to bring up their children.

Six women assisted Oberlin in his difficult task, amongst others, his wife and the servant maid Louise Scheppler, later awarded the 'Prize of Virtue' by the Paris Academy. After leaving the school the children were sent out to the surrounding villages to spread their knowledge, like little apostles. And so infant schools started to develop everywhere. On his death Oberlin left behind a community of orderly, pious and enlightened families.

This story about Oberlin can also be found in the historical records of English and American infant school education (Forest, 1929; Hadow Report, 1933). His was supposedly the first school for young children but, in fact, long before 1770 'dame schools', 'play schools' and 'women's schools' were in existence. Why, then, is Oberlin's school famous for being the first infant school, and why this near mythical story of its origins?

The older versions of the story are very similar to the revelation story inspired by Christians. Oberlin had a 'revelation' and his ex-pupils spread the message like 'little apostles'. It is a story that is intended to act as an example for the benefit of mankind.

Three themes are apparent in the contents of the story. In the first place the theme of *social reforms*: Oberlin aims for prosperity, civilization and a religious awareness for an ignorant, impoverished and rough community. The second theme concerns the *earliest years of childhood*. The children play a key role in the process of social reform because they are easier to educate than adults. Children are given a special place, the school, which protects them from the hard adult world. They receive an education specially suited to their 'nature' – for instance, the very youngest are allowed to play.

The third theme is about the *(ambiguous) position of women and mothers*. As those responsible for the children's upbringing, the women are also given a key role in the social reforms. Through this, the societal meaning of motherhood is changed. In the first place bringing up children as a specific activity was disconnected from the other activities carried out by women. Oberlin's example was the girl at the spinning wheel, who, without any clear pedagogical intention, had educated the children through her songs. However, in the school, women are exempted from other activities: their only job and aim is to bring up and educate the children.

Secondly, a distinction is made between ignorant mothers and those women/mothers with special pedagogic talents. For the latter group, the chosen, this means recognition and the possibility of practising a profession outside the home and family. It is no coincidence that in the tale the name of one of the women is mentioned, Louise Scheppler; this points to individuality and social status.

Those chosen to be educators also had the task of educating the mothers. This brought about an ambiguous situation with regard to the mothers. On the one hand mothers were given more time by the school, enabling them to do more work on the land and in the home, but, on the other hand, the ideal being put across by the educators at the school was that of the 'ever-available mother', in a space especially created for children. The fact that mothers were unable to care for their children due to their activities, was used to realize an educational ideal in which educators offered the children their exclusive attention. All this was carried out under the leadership of a man.

These three themes in Oberlin's tale – the idea of social reform, the importance of the first years of childhood, and the (ambiguous) position of women and mothers – are all themes that, even now, still dictate the discussions on child-care centres, the education of young children and motherhood. However, the manner in which these themes have become manifest through the years is not always the same. Sometimes one theme was dominant, then another; sometimes the role they played was barely apparent. But, together these three themes have directed not only pedagogic philosophy, but also the later developmental psychology.

SOCIO-POLITICAL BACKGROUNDS

At the start of the nineteenth century schools for young children were set up experimentally in various places in Europe and

America. The pedagogical experiments were set up or financed by liberal aristocrats and enlightened citizens in order to combat poverty and immorality amongst the population. Although these experiments were geographically distant from one another, there are indications of contact, through correspondence and travel (Singer, 1989).

The first experiments with philanthropic infant schools found little following. The breakthrough came in England, after the great industrialist Robert Owen founded the New Lanark Infant School in Scotland in 1816. Owen put his ideals down on paper and proceeded to visit influential monarchs, statesmen and academics in different European countries and in the United States; he also visited Oberlin's and Pestalozzi's experiments (Owen, 1967). According to Owen's theories, the infant schools formed the cornerstone of the social reforms which were to eradicate 'evil' from society: specifically the poverty, unemployment, crime and immorality of the fast-growing cities. In a number of places in Britain, people took up the initiative and founded infant schools, which prompted a stream of publications on education for young children. In the British infant schools, visitors from Germany, Italy, Hungary, Austria, Switzerland, Sweden and the Netherlands found support for their own, often much older initiatives. The United States did not lag behind in this enterprise.

The success of infant schools after 1820 is often associated with the industrialization and the rapid development of an impoverished proletariat; with the separation of paid employment and family life; and with the rise of enlightenment philosophy (Clarke, 1985; McCann and Young, 1982; Pence, 1986; Shapiro, 1985; Van Rijswijk-Clerkx, 1981). All three of these backgrounds are most clearly apparent in the English infant school movement.

In Great Britain, the process of industrialization started in 1750, more than a century before that in the United States or the Netherlands. This process went hand in hand with horrific forms of child labour in factories, and child neglect, as mothers and elder sisters went to work in the factories. The first half of the nineteenth century saw a rapid growth of industrial towns. Manchester grew from 85,000 to 400,000, Leeds from 53,000 to 172,000 and Bradford from 13,000 to 104,000 inhabitants. The poorer areas of these industrial towns were characterized by bad housing, overcrowding, lack of sanitary facilities, infected water and poor food. They were centres of epidemic infections such as scarlet fever and diphtheria, which claimed many victims, especially amongst the children. During the entire nineteenth century, child mortality in England was approximately 150 per 1,000 children.

The city environment meant a break with the old ties and traditions of the country. The separation between the place of work and the home made it impossible for working parents to take care of or keep an eye on their children at home. Where mothers went out to work this was generally a financial necessity. There was no choice between being a housewife or going out to paid employment. From the first official statistics in which married women were included (published in England in 1851), it is apparent that 24 per cent of married women were in paid employment of some sort.

Among the middle classes fear grew for the neglected children growing up without discipline. The first period of enthusiasm for infant schools came at the same time as the dramatic increase in child crime (McCann, 1966). Observers from this period claimed that at least one-third of the children between the ages of 7 and 13 never attended school, and occupied themselves with gambling and pickpocketing. The middle classes sought ways of eliminating this threat, and infant schools seemed to offer a way of replacing parental control.

Industrialization also increased the difference between rich and poor. Whilst poor mothers were forced to leave their homes and children to work for a living, the women from the middle and upper classes were finding it increasingly difficult to find employment in order to live independently, or to practise any sort of profession outside the family. Women's right to any form of higher education had to be fought for during the entire nineteenth century. Women were denied any admission to political functions or direct political influence. The family and home was the place where women belonged, and where 'men' did not work. Men and women were forced to live in different worlds. This was not only in practical terms (because of the areas in which they were allowed to be active), but also because of the ideas about masculinity and femininity at the time. Femininity was associated with sacrifice, chastity, tender caring, a feeling for the community, emotionality and maternity. This coincided with the idea that young children needed the maternal breast, maternal love and maternal care above all else. Not that all children from the middle and upper classes actually received this. The system of 'nannying' (hiring 'live-in' women from the lower classes to look after the children), was widespread in England (Gathorne-Hardy, 1972).

Social tension caused by poverty and industrialization make it understandable that the upper classes felt the need to find ways of controlling the situation; but why did they think that infant schools were the answer? This brings me to the Enlightenment philosophy. From the sixteenth century on, a new world image developed amongst European intellectuals. The Protestants broke away from the unity of Christianity and the moral authority of the Church, and demanded the separation of Church and state, and the freedom to choose on questions of belief. Descartes's 'I think, therefore I am' opened the way to a new understanding of self, personal consciousness and individual autonomy. The rationalism of the eighteenth century started a process of secularization of human belief: humanity must be enlightened by reason. Fed by successes within the natural sciences (Newton), the entire creation – man, animals and plants – was explained as a machine that works according to certain unequivocal laws. Knowledge of the natural laws of social existence would make the social order controllable. Enlightenment philosophers believed that society could be 'made', and they rejected the traditional Christian ideas of providence, predestination or higher divine powers leading human history. In the future, social progress and moral perfection would be within reach of the 'rational man'. Although within the Christian tradition the dogma of original sin was almost uncontested, the Enlightenment philosophers started from the principle that a human being comes into the world innocent and empty, and is by nature gifted with reason. If a person is bad and commits evil, this is caused in the first place by a bad upbringing and corrupt people in power. The source of 'evil' is not sought 'in' man, but in the environment which gives the wrong examples, and where bad habits are taught, and ignorance, poverty and corruption dominate.

A deep-rooted optimism in people's educability formed the core of Enlightenment philosophy, but not all doubts about man and his sinful nature were removed by this attitude. Great pedagogic philosophers of the Enlightenment, such as Locke and Rousseau, struggled with the question of the balance between freedom and the individual and authority, and the question of the relationship of the individual and society. They sought ways of shaping and controlling the potential evil in man or society (see Chapter 3). How to educate people well became a central problem.

From the end of the eighteenth century a great number of institutions were developed for the elevation of humanity – public education, mental homes and prisons – all with an educative aim (Foucault, 1967, 1979). Pedagogic textbooks were published, with advice for the family upbringing in the middle classes. Compared with popular education and the enlightened writings for family upbringing, the infant school is a relative late-comer to enlightened pedagogic philosophy.

Thus far, we have set out the general background to the infant school movements in Western countries. However, there were great national differences. For instance, in the Netherlands it was not industrialization, but rather the fear of impoverished masses that played a large part. In various countries there was, to a greater or lesser degree, resistance to infant schools. People felt that the family upbringing would be eroded, and mothers from the working class did not feel inclined to hand their children over to some 'strange' institution. I will return to this later.

UTOPIAN AND PRAGMATIC AIMS

The pedagogic aims of the infant school varied from Utopian (the 'new moral world') to pragmatic (crime prevention or preparation for popular education).

The formation of character

For Robert Owen, the infant school fitted conveniently into his total plan for the new moral world. As part-owner of cotton mills in New Lanark, Owen introduced far-reaching social reforms. He introduced improvements in the living and working conditions of his workers. He prohibited work by children under the age of 7, and founded an 'Institute for the Formation of Character', the infant school for children from the age of 1 or 2. He wanted to remove children from parental authority as young as possible, at an age when they had not yet been formed or spoiled.

Owen was an enlightened pedagogue and an outstanding industrialist. Amongst his friends were enlightened intellectuals such as Jeremy Bentham, R.L. Edgeworth and enlightened Scottish moral philosophers and political economists, who endeavoured to give the study of man and society an empirical basis. In Owen's work all enlightened philosophical streams of his time can be found: millenarianism, philanthropy, socialism, communitarianism (Harrison, 1968).

Owen was convinced of a 'rational socialism' founded without social conflicts and oppositions. Poverty, crime and laziness were, according to him, caused by ignorance. Everyone could be made content by the material welfare made possible by industrialization, and by a rational education from birth (Owen, 1967: 104–6). Owen believed that man is in essence good, and that children cannot help it if they learn bad habits. 'Has the infant any means of deciding who, or of what description shall be its parents, its playmates, or those from whom it shall derive its habits and its sentiments?' (Owen, 1967: 346). Who and what you are is only the result of your upbringing, Owen told his readers:

> Every day will make it more clear and evident that the character of man, is, without a single exception, always formed for him; that it may be, and is, chiefly, created by his predecessors; that they give him, or may give him, his ideas and habits, which are the powers that govern and direct his conduct. Man, therefore, never did, nor is it possible he ever can, form his own character.
>
> (Owen, 1967: 77)

According to Owen the family was a breeding place for group egoism and anti-social behaviour.

> The children within these dens of selfishness and hypocrisy are taught to consider their own individual family their own world, . . . With these persons it is *my* house, *my* wife, *my* children, or *my* husband; *our* estate; and *our* children . . . *our* property. . . . No arrangement could be better calculated to produce division and disunion in society.
>
> (Owen, cited in Taylor, 1983: 39)

As well as this, parents acted too much from irrational motives. According to Owen, education and upbringing should be a collective responsibility. Only then could rationality triumph.

Until about 1850 a flourishing Owenite movement existed in both Britain and the United States. The movement's activities included organizing trade unions, public meetings, communal experiments, and a feminist struggle for equal rights for women (Taylor, 1983). But Owen was a controversial figure because of his atheism, socialism and his struggle against family and marriage. After about 1820, he was reviled within the infant school movement, and completely written out of history. The English socialists were the first to rediscover his ideas in approximately 1880. The pedagogues followed in 1920. However, it took another 130 years, until 1983, before the Owenite–feminist theory and practice were drawn out of obscurity by Barbara Taylor.

EDUCATING TOWARDS VIRTUE AND OBEDIENCE

Most of the advocates of the infant school movement in Britain, such as Wilderspin and Stow, were not interested in the fundamental changes in human nature and society sought by Owen. Their primary concern was to put an end to certain practices that posed a threat to social stability. For example, Wilderspin's much-translated and reprinted textbook *Infant Education; or, Remarks on the Importance of Educating the Infant Poor* started with a reference to crime and immorality. 'Scenes that cause human nature to shudder' he associated with education for young children. Infant schools were to make prisons unnecessary (McCann, 1966). Crime prevention was also given as one of the most important motives for infant school education in Italian and French textbooks of the period (Forest, 1929: 69–82). In the Dutch textbooks 'well-organized infant schools' were also recommended as a 'prevention against evil' (Singer, 1989: 65).

The most important aim of the infant school was moral training: telling the truth, obedience and docility, honesty, decency, propriety and good appearance, order and submission, mutual courtesy and politeness, and being industrious. Religious education also played a large part. The Churches discovered infant schools as a pedagogic instrument.

According to Borstelman (1983), in the perfecting of man religion formed a feeding ground for two opposing visions on education. On the one hand he places the pedagogues who rejected the idea of original sin. Opposite them he places the Christian conservatives, who defended the doctrine of original sin, but who, through education, hoped to banish or at least control evil. Both streams confronted each other at times, as in

Britain and the Netherlands in the 1860s (McCann and Young, 1982; Coronel, 1864). In Britain, for instance, Wilderspin wanted to educate the children to accept religion through love and to achieve this in a playful, childlike manner. On the other hand, orthodox Protestants considered that religious dogmas should be etched on the mind, and the will should be broken in order to fight innate evil. From the 1840s onward the orthodox Protestants' opinions dominated in the English infant school movement.

In the Netherlands the Church's grip on infant schools probably did not lead to such strict and conservative views. 'Suffer the little children to come unto me' became one of the most frequently quoted pronouncements in textbooks for infant schools. But further,the emphasis was on obedience stemming from love, and faith in the Creator. According to Kruithof (1982), in the Netherlands the orthodox and liberal Christian had great differences of opinion about the root of evil, but scarcely any difference in their practical pedagogic advice.

PREPARATION FOR POPULAR EDUCATION

A third and very influential aim of the infant school movement was connected to the developments within another branch of Enlightenment philosophy: popular education. The new 'enlightened' didactic methods made high demands on the children's (self-) discipline. Because of this, very young children were no longer suited to the infant school. Besides, the need for a 'pre-school' developed, in order to prepare children for a more disciplined school life.

Until the end of the eighteenth century, classical instruction and group discipline in education were barely known. The children worked individually, and came in turn to repeat their lessons to the teacher. The children were together in one class-room, with ages varying from 2 to 12 years. There was no strict, orderly system. For this reason the younger children did not form a separate problem requiring specific attention.

However, in the eyes of the enlightened school reformers, this method of working was chaotic and inefficient. They sought ways of teaching more children, more lessons, in a shorter time. In Britain until 1840 the solution was sought in the 'monitorial system', or the Bell-Lancaster system (Jones and Williamson,

1979). Within this system the more advanced pupil (the 'monitor'), passed the lessons on from the teacher to small groups of less advanced pupils. In this way one teacher could instruct any number from 100 to 1,000 pupils. All the children were gathered into one space in groups of ten to twenty, and arranged in rows or squares under the direct supervision of the 'monitor'. The teacher superintended the entire classroom. This classroom had the appearance of a military exercise ground, with groups of exercising children being commanded by 'monitors' blowing on whistles and shouting commands, while the teacher supervised the whole proceedings like an army general. But the 'monitorial system' aimed at more than just repression or discipline through external violence. Corporal punishment was discouraged, and good behaviour was rewarded with cards that could be handed in at the end of the week and exchanged for money. Disobedient children were punished by working on their sense of shame (hanging a board round their neck), by exclusion and by isolation. The children were supposed to learn moral principles, become motivated and thus need no external force.

It will no doubt be clear that it was not easy to fit young children into this sort of regime. They were still unresponsive to the reward and punishment system, too lively, and not yet able to be 'monitors'. Besides which, they distracted the older children with their crying, noise and undisciplined behaviour. In other countries such as the Netherlands, but also in Britain after 1840, the classical system of education was introduced (Van Setten, 1982), the main aim still being more efficiency. The previously arranged lessons had to be systematically dealt with by the teacher, and passed on to a classroom of pupils, who had all reached a similar level. By using a phased (understandable) teaching process, the pupils' interest was to be aroused, and the boring routine work of the old school system could be done away with. New reading methods were introduced, and the use of visual material was encouraged.

Although the classical education was less military and strict than the 'monitorial' system, it became apparent that even here the young children were difficult to supervise. Classical education turned the school into a *quiet school*, and young children are difficult to keep quiet. Quite apart from which, learning to understand, as a class, placed high demands on the children's ability to concentrate.

Turning young children away from popular education posed new problems. Who would look after them? The fear grew that older children would be kept at home to look after the younger ones. Absence from school was seen as a great problem, and there was, as yet, no compulsory education. Educational reformers thus pleaded for infant schools for the very young (Szreter, 1964; Silver and Silver, 1974).

There were more arguments in favour of this. According to the teachers, a great many children in the first class had not learnt discipline at home. Mothers were blamed for the disappointing school results and the problems of maintaining order. Children were arriving at school already spoilt, whilst their enormous capacity to learn, inherent in all young children, was being left unused. Lord Brougham, a radical advocate of public education and infant schools, spoke powerfully on this subject in the House of Lords in 1835:

> Schools in the country are only open to children too far advanced in years. . . . Whoever knows the habits of children at an earlier age than that of six or seven – the age at which they generally attend infant schools . . . is well aware of their capacity to receive instruction long before the age of six. . . . His attention is more easily aroused, his memory is more retentive, bad habits are not yet formed, nor is his judgement warped by unfair bias. Good habits may be easily formed.
>
> (Cited in Forest, 1929: 48)

FAMILY, MATERNITY AND THE INFANT SCHOOL

Long before the infant school developed there was a great deal of interest in the education of young children in the educated and better-off families. From the middle of the eighteenth century, a growing stream of publications led to a greater understanding of the meaning of early childhood and maternity (Clarke, 1985; Kruithof, 1982; Wishy, 1968). Breast-feeding was recommended, as well as more enlightened ideas about hygiene, physical care and children's play and exercise. The unhygienic, stiff swaddles were rejected, as well as the use of sleep-inducing drinks like the sugar-lump drenched in gin. People started to see love and an emotional tie between the parents and the child as being the most important basis of upbringing and education. How can the interest in infant schools be reconciled with the praise given to family upbringing and maternal care?

According to Clarke (1985), the rise of the maternal and family ideology in the middle classes formed an important impulse for the development of infant schools for the lower class. The sight of large numbers of children on the streets with no parental supervision became an offence against standards created by an ideology which placed the protection of mother and child against the dangers of the outside world in a central position. The more beautiful the ideal, the worse everything seems that does not conform to this. A similar association probably moved the Dutch pedagogue Betje Wolff, when she wrote the following in 1780: 'Yes my heart bleeds when I see how sad, how depressingly sad is the education of the most poverty stricken in their intolerably squalid shacks' (Von Wolzogen-Kuehr, 1920: 5). The charity work carried out by middle class women in infant schools was seen as an extension of their maternal care within the family, to maternal care of society; as a fitting way of exceeding the limits of the family circle (Block, 1978; De Bie and Fritschy, 1985).

In many textbooks, Dutch as well as English, French and Italian, infant schools were justified by pointing out the ideal of the family upbringing (Singer, 1989). The parent or mother–child relationship was supposedly the basis of the upbringing – but then objections followed. If the mother had to work outside the home, many children would remain uncared for and unprotected, resulting in fatal accidents and moral decay. But, even if mothers stayed at home, there was still a great deal lacking, either due to ignorance and poverty in the families of the poor; or due to the flightiness of the mothers or the tyranny of nannies in middle-class families.

The criticism that infant schools would weaken the parent–child relationship was denied. Parents would always remain responsible for the time spent outside school, and for clothing and feeding their children. 'Hard cruel parents', who were temporarily relieved of their little 'teasers', would see the 'open, clear-eyed face of the returning child' and therefore become better parents (*Iets*, 1842). Good parents would not lose their child's love through the infant school: 'In the human heart, also in the heart of our youngest, there is enough space to love others as well as you' (*Iets*, 1842). Apart from this, the children of today were the educators of tomorrow; through the love and care they received in the infant school, they themselves would become better parents. In a number of textbooks the infant school was seen as a form of *family replacement, and correction of the deplorable shortcomings of the family.* The criticism of families and mothers from the lower classes is fully emphasized. The more the infant school treads the ground of family upbringing, the more the textbook writers emphasize that the infant school only strengthens family upbringing.

However, not all textbook writers make such a distinction between 'good' and 'bad' families. For example, the Dutchman Mulder (1827) felt that there should be infant schools for all children rich or poor, because (and he cited a certain pedagogue in agreement):

Parents cannot and may not have their children around them all day. In many cases the wife has to help the husband by carrying out useful duties, in which young children are a nuisance. It is also necessary, when keeping children occupied all day, to have at one's disposal a certain amount of good humour, liveliness and jollity; qualities that few mothers have or can give. . . . Therefore it is a double need, for parents and for children, that strangers can take over the care and responsibility.

(Mulder, 1827: 23)

But Mulder was an exception. A third justification for infant schools as far as family upbringing was concerned was more often heard: the infant school was supposedly an *extension of the family and a form of preparatory education.* In this argument, a distinction was made between daily care and upbringing on the one hand, and more systematic education in groups, on the other. For instance, in the Dutch textbooks it was stated that mothers did not offer their infants sufficient knowledge of numbers. Mothers did not adhere to Pestalozzi's guidelines (Prinsen, 1820). By offering preparatory education, the efficiency of popular education could be magnified.

DAME SCHOOLS AND INFANT SCHOOLS

Up to now we have heard only the opinions of textbook writers and theoreticians. What did the mothers think of the infant schools? As in many other areas, we know very little from the perspective of those who did not write. In the Netherlands there has been no research at all in this field, and only little in Britain (Leinstor-Mackay, 1976; Roberts, 1972; Turner, 1970).

In order to understand the parents' position we must keep two points in mind. In the first place, infant schools set up by philanthropists were developed *for*, but not *by* the working class. The condescending attitude was not always appreciated by the parents. According to Roberts (1972), infant schools were in fact far from popular amongst the working class of Britain, in spite of the obvious advantages they offered: the parents' contribution was low, and working mothers very obviously needed child-care, but British infant schools were rarely full. Distrust and hostility towards charity made parents unreceptive to advice and meddling in upbringing by 'authority'. Mothers sometimes protested against the strict school hours and rules, which stated that children should attend school in clean clothes, with hair cut short. The new education methods in the infant schools – singing, exercise, talking – also called forth parents' resistance. They felt that children should go to school to learn instead of play. It is quite possible that the infant schools were most attractive to the better-off amongst the working class.

In the second place, when trying to understand the parents' attitude towards well-organized infant schools, we must remember that there was an alternative: the *dame schools or little children's school*. In the dame schools no demands were made. They were run by a woman from their own class with whom they made a personal financial arrangement. The picture we are given of these dame schools in English and Dutch literature is extremely black: dark, damp classrooms, overcrowded with children, vermin, foul stenches, boredom and soul-destroying activities, under the supervision of a dilapidated old woman, herself hardly able to read or write. However, this picture was mainly created by notorious opponents of the dame schools in their arguments for infant schools set up by philanthropists.

In her research, Leinster-Mackay (1976) shows that many rich and famous English men and women actually attended a dame school in their youth, and in their memoirs they write very positively about them. Probably not all dame schools were bad. There are also a number of positive descriptions of Dutch dame schools (Van Essen, 1985). According to Roberts (1972), the significance of the dame school – a non-institutionalized form of

education and free profession for women – is greatly undervalued in English history. According to him there were more
dame schools than infant schools. It is therefore questionable
whether the mothers were forced to use dame schools because of
the lack of infant schools, as so often stated by Dutch authors
(Clerkx, 1985).

These doubts about the bad picture so often painted of the dame
schools should not be interpreted as a total repudiation of un-
favourable descriptions. Undoubtedly there were many bad dame
schools. But the living and working conditions of working-class
families would not have been much better. And, how about the
practice in well-organized infant schools? Coronel was unable to
find sufficient words with which to revile the dame school, but at the
same time he had very little good to say about the well-organized
infant schools' in Amsterdam. Even so, his proposals for improvement were directed towards the latter form of education.

INFANT SCHOOLS, A BOTTLENECK OF INTERESTS

At the beginning of the nineteenth century infant schools
promised to provide a solution to various socio-political
problems. First, the infant school set up by a philanthropist was
intended to intervene in the education of the poor. By taking
children away from the (destructive) parental milieu, crime, immorality and lack of religious background could all be countered.
In the second place, the new demands being made within public
education cast a shadow on the future of education for the very
young: the need for care for infants who no longer fitted into
public education; the need for preparatory education that could
not be sufficiently given in the family. Apart from this, the infant
schools were based on the mothers' need for care for infants
because of their work or other responsibilities; compared to other
motives, this one is mentioned less often.

The well-organized infant school partly fitted in with the much
older tradition of parents sending their young children to little
children's schools, or dame schools. But, it was also partly a break
away from tradition, inasmuch as the intention was to educate
the (future) parents/mothers through the children, and thus to
elevate society.

There was also resistance to what was seen as meddling in
family upbringing. Parents were not always grateful for the inter-

ference from infant schools. Financiers had their doubts. Advocates made lengthy statements about why the infant school would not damage family life. They emphasized two differences that, even today, are influential in the philosophy behind care and education outside the family. They distinguished between 'good' and 'bad' families. The infant school would be like a good mother and give the children the care they were lacking at home. Beside this, a distinction was made between 'care' (at home) and 'preparatory education' (at school). Infant schools would offer either 'preparatory education' or 'family replacement education' for the children from 'bad families'. This way some *grip and control could be exercised on family education without undermining its value.*

Chapter 3

The power of first impressions

The first attempts to design a child-centred pedagogy

> It is a mother's duty to do within the family circle that which
> cannot be done during lessons at school; to give to each child
> individually, the attention the school cannot give, because
> there it is engulfed by the mass; to let her heart speak in the
> situations where only the heart can be the best judge; to achieve
> through love that which can never be achieved by power.
>
> (Pestalozzi, 1956)

A SOCIALLY 'EMPTY' SPACE

At the start of the nineteenth century the infant school could be
seen as a socially 'empty' space. The space was socially empty
because at that time there were no pedagogic traditions for
working with young children in groups, and also because the
children were excluded from the adult world by the school walls.
The contents of education – morals, habits, knowledge of the
(sub-) culture in which children grew up – could not be taught at
school in direct contact with older children and adults. Not only
the rules to which children had to adhere, but also the entire
learning experience had to be specially designed for this
children's world. The first pioneers of infant school education
had no easy task. What does one do with fifty, 100 or even 400, 2-
to 5-year-olds, packed together in one classroom? McCann described the almost traumatic first experience of the Englishman
Wilderspin, who was later to write a number of influential textbooks (McCann, 1966).

The first morning thirty-eight children were brought to
Wilderspin's infant school. As the mothers left, the entire group
burst into tears crying, 'Mummy, Mummy'! Wilderspin's wife

endeavoured to calm the children, but was forced to leave the classroom as it all became too much for her. Wilderspin also fled, exhausted by his efforts, the fear and noise. He left behind a mass of screaming children kicking at the door. In desperation, Wilderspin grabbed his wife's hat with colourful ribbons, perched it on top of an old mop and rushed back into the classroom. To his astonishment the children stopped crying. Before total chaos could break out again he had an inspiration and yelled: 'Now we are going to play "ducks" and I'm the big duck'. All the children started to quack in chorus. After that they played 'hen and chickens', and before they knew where they were it was twelve o'clock. Wilderspin's first attempt at 'learning through play', using a child-centred method, was born from necessity. But it was to take another century before the doll's corner, building corner, dressing-up boxes, puzzles and educational toys were discovered to fill the 'emptiness' of the classroom and playground.

This chapter is about the first attempts to develop a pedagogy for young children. At the time the infant schools came into existence there were theories by enlightened pedagogues about *upbringing in the family*, but simultaneously, there were theories about *educating older children at school*. The theories about the pedagogy in infant schools contained elements of both theoretical domains.

THE VIEWS OF ENLIGHTENED PEDAGOGUES ON YOUNG CHILDREN AND FAMILY UPBRINGING

Comenius, Locke, Rousseau and Pestalozzi all belonged to the school of thought that laid the foundations for an enlightened pedagogy from the seventeenth century. They had in common their idea of using the child's spontaneous play, its curiosity, talent for mimicry, and need for activity in the child's education. The 'child's nature' should not be misformed. They rejected the idea of 'sin' in newborn babies. Young children did not need to be saved from sin by strict discipline and parental authority. In other words: *within each child is the potential for good*. On the one hand enlightened pedagogues wanted to free the child from external authority and traditional manners of upbringing, but on the other hand they sought new ways of limiting the child's freedom, and creating a new balance between freedom and commitment (Wishy, 1968). How could the pedagogue help to develop the child's potential good?

The search for new pedagogic techniques was related to the rise of new theories about power (Clarke, 1985; Foucault, 1979). Before the Enlightenment, power was supposedly something visible, something that had to be applied externally. Wasn't it true that everyone had a tendency to evil because of original sin? This could, therefore, only be controlled by external forces. From the end of the eighteenth century, the idea that power must be based on shared values, general interests and an agreement between individual citizens (workers, women and children excepted), gained ground. This new view of power presupposed an individual with the self-discipline necessary to maintain the balance between individual and communal interests. *The rational human being was the key to a better and more democratic community.* Moreover, the general belief was that self-discipline and rationality could be developed by education.

According to enlightened pedagogues, education should be directed towards internalizing rules, values, standards and knowledge; towards an individual who is independently able to judge between good and evil, truth and falsehood, and independently able to acquire knowledge. The basis for this education would have to be laid in the earliest years of childhood, as what is learnt at a very young age is taken for granted and does not call forth resistance. Besides which, at a later age it is very difficult to change the bad habits learnt when very young. In other words: *the pedagogue is responsible for bringing the ideal community closer to realization.*

How could the basis for a reasonable and democratic human being be laid in early childhood? Intensive contact between those responsible for upbringing and the child would seem to be a condition for this. The 'child's natural development' had to be followed, and for this reason 'knowledge of children' was very important. According to Locke, 'habit forming' was the key. Rousseau opposed this, and said that discipline should be aroused 'naturally' and 'spontaneously', whilst others such as Comenius and Pestalozzi felt that self-discipline was born through maternal love.

The demands of permissiveness

The *School of Infancy* (*Mother School* was the original title) (1630) by Comenius is one of the oldest books on early education, based on the phases of child development. Like many educators after him, Comenius compared the work of the pedagogue to that of a gardener. Parents should restrict, water, cut and nurture the budding plant. In the daily contact with the mother or nanny, the child learns: 'Look, that's a bird, cat, calf, and so on', and 'What's that? What's this called? Why is that?' (Comenius, 1963: 39). The more freely the child is able to move, the better it will sleep and grow, and the fresher and quicker his body and spirit will become. Therefore safe areas with continuous supervision must be created.

According to Comenius, children under the age of 6 do not belong at school. They need more personal and individual attention than a teacher is able to give within a group. Their brains are not 'stabilized', according to Comenius, and why shouldn't we be satisfied with those things a child can safely and playfully learn at a 'mother school"?

Locke's 'Some thoughts concerning education', of 1690, was originally intended as advice for a father he knew, on how to bring up his son. The mother is barely mentioned by Locke. According to Locke, the child comes into the world as a *tabula rasa*. The first impressions were of great and lasting influence, and he felt the earliest habit forming to be of crucial importance.

> Pray remember, children are not taught by rules, which will be always slipping out of their memories. What you think necessary for them to do, settle in them by an indispensable practice, as often as the occasion returns; and, if be possible, make occasions.
>
> (Locke, 1964: 42)

Habits learnt by children when very young, advised Locke, appear to them natural and are taken for granted. They don't know any better, and that prevents struggles. Apart from this, parents should take into account the individual peculiarities of their children. Observe your children, Locke advised, and determine their capabilities and limitations. Use their natural tendency towards imitation, curiosity and play. And never try to combat the sort of naughty behaviour that will, in time, disappear anyway. Locke's view was that virtuous and excellent people will, of their own accord, resist unreasonable behaviour, and that this should be learnt while very young. For this reason he was against spoiling children. Young children were expected to accept their parents' authority completely. Only later could a more friendly relationship become possible.

Rousseau was more radical than Locke. In *Emile*, first published in 1762, Rousseau rejected any form of training, habit forming or academic knowledge. Authority and human institutions were supposedly suffocating human nature without giving anything in return. For this reason Emile was brought up in quarantine until the age of 25, protected from all harmful influences from the adult community around him, in order to be able to develop 'naturally'. During the first years of life the mother plays the most important role, according to Rousseau, but under the supervision of the real pedagogue, the father. 'In the same way that the real nurturer is the mother, so the real governor is the father' (Rousseau, 1983:72). Mothers should breast-feed and care for the physical needs of their child, and apart from that leave the child free to move about at will and make its own discoveries. Rousseau realized that this was asking a great deal of mothers. A baby tightly wrapped in swaddles can safely be left in a corner, without demanding any further attention. 'A child growing up in freedom will have to be watched continuously' (Rousseau, 1983: 67).

Contrary to Locke, Rousseau felt that rigid rules for eating and sleeping should be resisted. The foundations of a free man are laid by 'allowing his body to retain the natural habits, by enabling him to remain always master of his own will, as soon as he has a will' (Rousseau, 1983: 84).

In spite of his view that the child is by nature good, Rousseau was obsessed by the destructive passions within man (Kessen, 1978: 158). Selfish passions and hatreds, such as jealousy, revenge and tyranny, were seen by him as a result of spoiling or commanding obedience. A spoilt child does not learn his own powerlessness and dependence: quite the opposite, it feels itself to be all-powerful, and demands that others satisfy its every need. For this reason Rousseau stated: teach the child to accept his natural powerlessness; teach the child that he is a 'child'. Give him real freedom, and the child will learn his own limitations and dependence on the governor by its confrontations with the (physical) environment. Make use of 'natural' punishments. The upbringer can give 'nature' some help by manipulating the child's environment. Thus, Emile's governor orders the gardener to destroy Emile's garden; through this Emile would learn about the right of ownership. The motivation to learn to read is aroused by giving Emile letters to read when, 'quite coincidentally', there was no one around to read them for him. Emile's environment appears to be natural, but in fact it is carefully planned.

Rousseau's ideal governor must observe his pupil carefully, and penetrate the most hidden corners of the child's soul. In this sense, Rousseau goes even further than Locke, who advocated a more open authority. The child's freedom and an invisible and impersonal power over the child go hand in hand in Rousseau's vision. 'Let your pupil always believe that he is the master, but in fact be the master yourself. No other subjection is so complete as that which keeps up the pretence of freedom; in such a way one can even imprison the will' (Rousseau, 1983: 130).

According to Kessen (1978), who doubted Rousseau's so-called love of children, Rousseau was trying to manipulate child behaviour, and can thus be seen as a predecessor of the later behaviourists, who researched methods of conditioning children's behaviour.

Maternal love and self-discipline

As far as Pestalozzi (1746–1827) was concerned, maternal love played a key role. In order to keep the mother's love, the child would abandon 'the passions that make it so unlovable' (Pestalozzi, 1956: 140). According to Pestalozzi, children, 'products of nature', are instinctively led by sensual pleasure, with no consciousness of good or bad. They are innocent. But, in order to grow into 'moral beings', they must develop a pure and moral power against the animal power.

As far as Pestalozzi is concerned, maternal love is the purest of human emotions, and the reflection of an even purer feeling: love and belief in the Creator, in whose hands rest the ultimate power of redemption. Without maternal love, the child's instinctive impulse would develop into 'a thousand imaginary and artificial needs; that would send us from one pleasure to another and eventually end in complete selfishness' (Pestalozzi, 1956, 140). In nine out of ten cases, murderers and thieves will have had a loveless childhood.

Pestalozzi warned against the use of punishment and prohibitions: 'Prohibition works as a stimulus to desire. Fear can never work as a moral force, it can only serve to stimulate the physical desire, and estrange and embitter the soul' (Pestalozzi, 1956: 78). Pestalozzi required mothers to be self-sacrificing and humble. A mother is an island of purity in a degenerate world.

> In a world of selfishness, it will rest upon her to lead the spontaneous tenderness of her child and to develop this into a source of goodness, that does not recoil from any self denial for a good cause, and finds no sacrifice too much'
>
> (Pestalozzi, 1956, 42)

According to Pestalozzi, mothers also fulfil a key role in the intellectual upbringing; she is the child's first teacher (Pestalozzi, 1956: 109). Her first lessons should be linked in a natural way to the child's play. She can draw the child's attention to things in the environment, and make it familiar with sounds and meanings. The child would learn from 'first-hand' experience. By this Pestalozzi meant not only sensual experiences, but also, with the mother's help, the discvovery of the internal meaning of things and their religious meaning. The school would then build upon what the mother had already taught the child.

Knowledge of natural development

Comenius, Locke, Rousseau and Pestalozzi all encouraged parents to observe and study child behaviour. The upbringing should not go against the 'child's nature', but make use of, and be mindful of, the phases and laws of development. From the end of the eighteenth century publications appeared in the Netherlands, Britain and the United States about the impulsive nature of the child. Is the child by nature good or bad? Does the will need to be broken? How can the impulsive nature be formed? Learning by play, the child's thirst for knowledge and need of activity. These are subjects mentioned (Bloch, 1974; Kessen, 1965; Verwoerd, 1986). Parents from the more liberal classes started observing their children in order to discover their 'nature', and sometimes wrote diaries on the development of their children (Dietrich, 1976). Pestalozzi kept a diary on his son, named Jean-Jacques after Rousseau. Robert Owen's good friends tried to educate their sons 'like Emile', and published their observations during this (failed) experiment (Edgeworth and Edgeworth, 1798). Alcott (one of the first Americans to experiment with infant school education), who also tried to design a 'natural' upbringing, published his diary about his daughter's first year (Strickland, 1973/74).

This interest in a pedagogy based on 'child knowledge' led in Germany to a blossoming empirical child psychology from 1750. Nowadays the rise of empirical development psychology is generally placed at the end of the nineteenth century, but the now mainly forgotten psychologists and educators such as Engel, Schwarz, Niemeyer, Kruger, Trap, Tetens, Campe and Tiedeman were all involved with empirical research into children's knowledge ability, observation, imaginative power, memory, language development, the origin of self-awareness, awakening, sleeping, dreaming and play (Singer, 1989).

Empirical findings on early childhood development were often explicitly coupled to moral pedagogic questions; for instance, by Mulder (1827), when he described the growing self awareness of children. According to Mulder their growing awareness of 'I' is linked to a 'pleasant impulse to sociability', 'a deep-rooted attachment to the mother', and to 'fear'. The latter is of great importance, according to Mulder. 'If one feels no fear one cannot feel dependent', and feels no fear of God. Fear of separation makes the child educable and prevents it turning into a 'beast of prey or a monster in human society'. Mulder probably put into words the moral background of our present day preoccupation with mother–child attachment (bonding) (see Chapters 6 and 8) which is no longer so explicit. One who is not bonded loses touch with God.

THEORIES ABOUT EDUCATION IN INFANT SCHOOLS

Comenius, Locke, Rousseau and Pestalozzi rejected formal education in groups for young children. Their ideas about the upbringing of young children were strongly related to the family situation, and probably at that time only applicable to the families of the liberal classes and enlightened aristocracy. In these circles there was time for intensive pedagogic contact between those responsible for upbringing and the child; there was time for observation and child studies. Also, the aim of this sort of upbringing coincided with the ideal of the free, democratic person with an internalized morality.

How did the infant school fit into this family-orientated philosophy? How did the theories for a family upbringing relate to
the theories for the infant schools?

Owen's group upbringing

Similar to the educators already mentioned, Owen wanted a
'natural upbringing', making use of the child's liveliness, urge to
play and thirst for knowledge. Owen felt that the community
should be responsible for the upbringing. This was related to his
ideas of communal living and socialism in an industrialized
society (see page 23). Owen promoted group upbringing, not
only for working-class children but for all children. He rejected
punishment, reward and competition because they disrupt the
community spirit. The children with more talent or rich parents
get all the rewards, whilst those less fortunate get the punishment. Only 'natural' punishment was allowed at the New Lanark
Infant School. 'Natural' punishment consisted of confronting the
children with the consequences of their behaviour for the welfare
of the group. Right from the start the following principle was
applied: 'Whatever, in its ultimate consequences, increases the
happiness of the community, is right; and whatever, on the other
hand, tends to diminish that happiness, is wrong' (R.D. Owen,
1968: 133). If a child does something wrong, it should not be
rejected, but handled with sympathy: we should sympathize
with the child that it cannot, yet, be reasonable.

From the age of 18 months the children attended the 'Institute
for the Formation of Character' for whole days. Under Owen's
direction, the children sang, danced and were played with.
Learning from books was absolutely forbidden. Their curiosity
must be stimulated by walks through gardens, orchards and
woods. Their questions and thirst for knowledge were to be taken
seriously in order to help them develop a rational character.
Every morning there was a programme of lessons for the
youngest, developed from their own experience. In the afternoon
the children played, about 100 children in the playground, supervised by just one girl, who, according to Owen's son Robert, with
less trouble, less punishment and more friendliness, managed to
maintain more order than many others were able to maintain in a
nursery with only two children (R.D. Owen, 1968: 146).

Instruction and harsh discipline

As has become clear from the previous chapter, very few advocates of the infant school system shared Owen's views. Their
primary concern was crime prevention in the lower classes, and a
form of preparatory education. This had consequences for the
development of a pedagogy and training techniques for young
children. Once again I have chosen Wilderspin as a representative
of this philosophy.

In Wilderspin we find not only elements of enlightened ideas
about a natural upbringing, but also elements from the instruc-
tional tradition of the elementary school (see page 26). Wilderspin
was also convinced that the teacher should start by studying the
child, and adapt to the laws of nature. His first experiences had
taught him that young children need gaiety, amusement and
physical exercise, and that they learn through sensory perception.
For this reason he thought playgrounds should be equipped with
building bricks, skipping ropes, trees for climbing and fruit trees.

But, contrary to Owen, Wilderspin felt that the infant school
should also offer a formal education in reading, writing, arithmetic, grammar, geography, natural history, singing and Bible
stories. He designed a large number of didactic accessories for
'playful learning', such as simple rhymes and verses, pictures and
a sort of (complicated) counting frame. He rejected completely
any mechanical learning of facts. However, in practice things
turned out differently. This was probably the result of what
Wilderspin himself called his most important discovery: the
'gallery'. The 'gallery' was an adaptation of the spatial organization of the 'monitorial system' for young children. The children
were given seats in ascending rows (a sort of amphitheatre),
enabling the teacher to instruct and watch all the children at the
same time. For the 'real' drilling and exercising, he designed
separate classrooms for ten to twenty children to be supervised
by one teacher. Because of this organization, the lessons degener-
ated into boring repetitions. Wilderspin was unable to convert his
ideas on 'natural learning' into a system suitable for large groups
of young children.

Similar to Owen, Wilderspin thought that discipline could not
be taught through punishment, or by imposing rules and
learning Bible texts. Children should learn 'living' rules, that they
could internalize. Wilderspin and Owen had different ideas on

how this could be realized. Owen advocated rationality by living in groups. Wilderspin, on the other hand, placed the teacher–pupil relationship in a key role: win the child's heart, and for love it will do everything you ask of it. If the children only obey out of fear, this will result in resistance and an aversion to the lessons. Another disciplining technique recommended by Wilderspin was public shaming. The disobedient child was questioned by the teacher in front of the entire school, and then the other children had to decide on a fitting punishment. This system was said to be instructive for all the children present.

Maternal love and 'object lessons'

Pestalozzi had a great influence on the pedagogic forming of infant schools in the Netherlands, and later also in Britain and the United States. Pestalozzi himself was against formal education for young children. Only mothers can

> Give to each child individually, the amount of attention that the school cannot give, because there it is engulfed by the mass; let her heart speak in the situations where only the heart can be the best judge; achieve through love, that which can never be achieved by power.
>
> (Pestalozzi, 1956: 109)

It is difficult to conceive a clearer argument for family upbringing. But how does that fit in with his influence on infant school education? The answer is simple: precisely because he calculates the mothers' significance to be so great, so his wish to interfere with that influence is great! Pestalozzi criticized mothers on the basis of the ideal image he himself had created. He sought ways of educating mothers. The next step, taking over the education, is only a small step if mothers do not seem to be receptive to correction. The infant school was often presented as an ideal mother for children who were being badly brought up (see page 30).

Various textbooks for infant schools were based on the *Buch der Mutter* (1803 – Dutch edition published 1804), that Pestalozzi had written especially for mothers. It is a method of instruction requiring that the verbal instructions given by the mother or teacher be accompanied by the child's direct experience of things.

The mother was supposed to carry out these exercises exactly according to the instructions. The method begins with exercises for discovering and naming the 'external parts' of the body: 'The body, the head, the face, the sides of the face, the right side of the face, the left side of the face, the back of the head, the skull' and so on – nine long pages (Pestalozzi, 1804, 1). In the second series of exercises, the mother had to point out to the child which parts of the body were next to, above or below the parts already learnt. And so it continued.

These exercises, called 'object lessons', were common in infant schools until well into the twentieth century. In textbooks, teachers were encouraged to give classical instructions in observation, comparison and differentiation, judgement and decision making, counting and measuring, speaking, reading and writing, and all in a playful manner. I will return later to the fact that these 'object lessons' were often far from playful.

Various textbook authors adopted Pestalozzi's ideas on maternal love. The teacher was supposed to guide and form the children with tender love and care, so that the feeling of love, gratitude and trust could develop in the children's hearts; particularly with regard to 'their Heavenly Father' and 'their parents, brothers and sisters, and all those with whom they came into contact' (Singer, 1989: 99).

Frightening children with horror stories, buying them off with sweets or the use of threats were all strictly forbidden, and quite unnecessary for maintaining order. The view of many was that withholding love was sufficient punishment for young children.

Punishment and reward, perhaps necessary in exceptional cases, were to be carried out quietly and out of earshot of the other children. Making an example of a child was always considered to be wrong, as it created a distance between the children, and suffocated their love for one another.

"Maternal love' thus functioned as a basis for moral and religious forming in infant schools. This was very different from Owen's pedagogy, based on ideas about rationality, equality in relationships between the children, and the communal group's interests, and also Wilderspin's pedagogy, based on ideas of a strict but just father, who wins the children's hearts and whose aim it was to bind the children to rules through 'child tribunals'.

THE 'PARROT METHOD'

There was probably a world of difference between the textbooks and daily practice during the first half of the nineteenth century. Observers of the period, with enlightened pedagogic ideas, were full of criticism. In England, Wilderspin declared disappointedly that the teachers were incapable of anything more than the 'parrot method'. Round about 1840 he was one of the most fervent critics of the impoverished and bookish practices to which many infant schools had fallen prey (McCann, 1966: 203). Embittered, he wrote about the practice of his method:

> It was never my intention to injure the young brain by over-exciting it, or to fill the memory with useless rubbish; yet this is done. I cannot help it. I have done and will do my best to prevent such a violation of the very first principles of infant teaching.
>
> (Stewart and McCann, 1967: 266)

Gloomy conclusions were drawn from the results of research carried out into the situation of Dutch small children's schools and infant schools:

> It was never observing and then following nature, but more often misjudging and misusing her; seldom forming characters, but more often repressing them. . . . The more and the faster one could overload the child's brain, the greater the satisfaction one seemed to predict for it. Learning was the main object, upbringing was of secondary importance; producing a show, searching for effects were the main aims of the infant school.
>
> (Coronel, 1864: 267)

The complaints about the 'misuse of children's nature' and 'fact learning' very probably have the following background. In the first place was the bad material circumstances: generally speaking the classrooms were too small, and the number of children too great. In the Netherlands, for instance, there were classrooms of 13 metres in length and 9 metres wide holding up to 450 children (Coronel, 1864: 151). There were no playrooms, and the outdoor playgrounds left a great deal to be desired. 'Playing' was often nothing more than 'gymnastic exercises' on the school bench: clapping hands, stamping feet, shaking heads, bowing to each other and so on.

Secondly, there was a lack of techniques for 'playful learning' in groups. This was already apparent in Pestalozzi's school. His theories were modern, but his 'object lessons' were boring and mechanical. After visiting Pestalozzi's school, Owen described it as follows: 'He [Pestalozzi] was doing, he said, all he could to cultivate the heart, the head, and the hands of his pupils. His theory was good, but his means and experience were very limited, and his principles were those of the old system' (Owen, 1967: 177). Resistance to the idea that the child was good by nature formed a third background. In Britain this was a thorn in the side of the orthodox Protestants, who, after 1840, gained much influence in infant school education. They valued piety, discipline, Bible knowledge and fear of hell-fire, rather than believing in the pedagogic value of playing and gaiety (McCann and Young, 1982: 167–82).

Finally, there was a rise in the attention given to school subjects. Parents were often not enthusiastic about children playing, they wanted them to learn something at school (Roberts, 1972: 156), and the elementary education inspectors emphasized the importance of preparatory education (Turner, 1970). In Britain, the infant schools were gaining value as an integral part of the popular education system. In 1870, infant school education was even included in the new Education Act. In the Netherlands, education for young children remained outside educational legislation until 1956. However, there was also a definite trend to more orientation towards elementary education from about 1850. This was apparent, amongst other things, from the adherence to school hours: from nine to twelve and from two to four o'clock in the winter, and from eight to twelve and from two to five o'clock during the summer. The very youngest children were excluded.

The idealism of the early years of infants' education, elevating society through education in infant schools, vanished. Little was left of the institute for the formation of the character that Owen had had in mind. Also, specifically in the Netherlands, the infant schools became less suitable for the children of working mothers, because of their shorter hours.

HOME IS BEST, EXCEPT . . .

The infant school pedagogics developed within a field of tension between the idealism of an enlightened (family) upbringing, the practical demands made by elementary education, and the traditional views on the upbringing of young children. The enlightened theories demanded new standards. What consequences did this have on the philosophy of family upbringing and infant schools? The founders of enlightened pedagogy, such as Comenius, Locke, Rousseau and Pestalozzi, distinguished between caring and education. The greater freedom for the child within the family was linked by them to more (invisible) control and interference by the pedagogue. *The pedagogue is placed in a social vacuum,* and nearly always only described in relation to the child. Household work was rarely mentioned, and if mothers had to work outside the home, this was regretted. Mothers who actually chose enjoyment rather than their children were reviled (Singer, 1989). From this standard of exclusive pedagogic attention, the pedagogic interest and the interest of child-care (for mothers with activities not directed towards the child), were defined as incompatible. It was probably because of this that the child-care function of the infant school for the children of working mothers was either undervalued or seen to be a necessary evil. There were a few, like Owen, who felt differently, but his philosophy has had little influence on the infant school movement.

The new education theories associated 'freedom' and 'natural' development with a new moral system. The child is seen as a *tabula rasa* (Locke), or to carry 'good' and 'rational powers' as its natural potential (Rousseau, Pestalozzi). The pedagogue was seen as the link between the potential ability of the child and the ideal society. In other words, the pedagogue was made responsible for attaining this ideal. Therefore, the pedagogues (mainly mothers), could be blamed for their children's 'bad behaviour'. It was not necessary to think about the social background to crime, such as poverty, or lack of future perspective.

Because the pedagogue was given a key role, he or she was *idealized on the one hand, and, on the other, watched like a hawk.* This was the reason for Pestalozzi's attempt to educate mothers. Continuing along these lines was the argument for infant schools to take over the entire upbringing of the child, especially if it was thought that the family was not fulfilling its task adequately, as in the lower classes.

These new standards, brought about by the enlightened theories, also produced an ambiguity towards preparatory education in infant schools. The educative aims were mainly taken from public education: (preparatory) reading, arithmetic, writing, geometry and rhyming. However, the standards for the teaching methods were taken from the ideals of a 'natural development' within the family, with a mother and one or two children. Because of this, at a theoretical level, the infant school found itself with a built-in conflict: *the transference of knowledge versus the following of 'nature'*. To this day people are still arguing from this same and, in my view, unfruitful and artificially created dilemma.

The sequence of family, infant school and public school was justified by the child's 'natural phases of development'. But the theoreticians were vague about when a child could be considered 'ripe' enough for the next phase. Besides, who is better able to carry out the method of 'natural' development – the mother, who can probably offer her child more personal attention, but who has no education, and a number of other daily activities as well as her child; or the infant school teacher, who has been educated, and has a great deal of time for the children, but has to spread her attention over a (large) group of children in a (small) space? Home is best, but can parents/mothers cope? *The line drawn between family, and education outside the family, today still remains a point of discussion.*

Chapter 4

Women's science
Froebel, the kindergarten movement and feminism

It is the mother's wisdom that can take humanity further than all the wisdom of men put together. But she has to know what she can do, and do what she knows. A new science has been discovered for her, designed by Froebel – the science of mothers, which can and must become the science of women generally.

(Elise van Calcar, 1879)

FEMINISM AND MOTHERHOOD (1850–1900)

The place is Amsterdam in 1860. On the stage is Elise van Calcar. She is speaking about 'the basis of human development'. This has been recorded in the history of feminism as the first lecture given by a Dutch woman in public. Her lecture also opened a new chapter in Dutch history on the upbringing of young children. Elise van Calcar introduced Friedrich Froebel and his ideas about child development, motherhood and play methods. Women were intended to have an educative mission. Froebel had designed a 'women's science' especially for them. The 'mothers' power' to make better people and a better society lay in the 'power of first impressions'.

In the second half of the nineteenth century the kindergarten movement was founded in Germany, the Netherlands, Britain, the United States and other Western countries. Within this movement women took leading positions; they combined pedagogic innovation with a feminist Utopia.

In this chapter the relationships will be analysed between Froebel's theories about the education and development of young children, and the feminist theories about 'spiritual motherhood' and the emancipation of women. What soci political goals did the Froebelians hope to achieve with tl kindergartens? How did they view the early development of the child? Why did women seek emancipation through motherhood?

FRIEDRICH FROEBEL (1782–1852)

Froebel's philosophy is rooted in the German idealism and romanticism of his time. He built further on the work already carried out by Comenius, Rousseau and Pestalozzi; the latter he knew, having worked with him for two years.

According to Froebel, the function and end of all things is to declare their divine essence, and thus to reveal God in what is external and transitory. He saw development as the unfolding of everything already present in the bud. In this he emphasized the developing child's own active role; the essence of the child was 'divine' – in other words, actively creative and self-realizing. According to Froebel, playing was the highest form of expression of the child's essence. Like Comenius, he described in detail how mothers could exercise their children's abilities: 'for instance, pointing to the light: – "There is the light," – taking it away: – "Now it's gone." – Or – "Father's coming", – "Father's gone" (Froebel, 1928: 147).

He linked these observations to vague mystical-symbolic reflections. The mother should help her child to experience the divinity of things. As far as Froebel was concerned, maternal love was a symbol and the highest manifestation of Divine unity. According to him the use of pressure or force in education destroyed the original purity and intrinsic laws. Behind every bad characteristic was a repressed good characteristic. Like Pestalozzi, he was of the opinion that selfishness was the result of a 'disturbed community feeling'. Invisible but ever present guidance through maternal love would make external discipline unnecessary.

However, like Pestalozzi, Froebel also shared the conviction that maternal love alone was not enough, because, he said, mothers often lack pedagogic abilities, knowledge and education. Only too often children are kept occupied with games and playing without any understanding of their true and deeper meaning.

HIS PEDAGOGY

In order to educate mothers he wrote *Mutter- und Koselieder* (Mother's Nursery Songs) (1843), a book of children's rhymes and games for mother and child, illustrated with rather sweet, romantic pictures. Froebel also designed the kindergarten for children from the age of 1 to 7. It was to be an institution for the 'cultivation of family life, and the forming of national life and even of all humanity' (Froebel, 1922: 56).

In the kindergarten, expert guidance could be given to mother and child. In order to achieve this Froebel worked out graduated exercises based on children's games, and designed simple educational apparatus, the 'gifts', to enable children to learn elementary laws of physical science and the eternal law of God. This method supposedly followed the child's 'natural' development, and therefore, had to be followed strictly. For instance, to start with, the first 'gift' had to be used: the ball – the symbol of unity. By experiencing the ball game, the child would learn about his own intrinsic unity, and learn concepts such as present and absent, search and find. After this children had to play with a wooden ball, a die and a cylinder; these were symbols of diversity, contrast and synthesis. The following 'gifts' were, amongst others, cubes divided into dice, square building bricks and mosaics. The children could not only build with these cubes, but also practise taste, regularity, perception and language. Further, Froebel advised all sorts of 'occupations' such as folding paper, plaiting mats, making clay figures, sewing, embroidery and drawing. Songs, stories, conversations, movement games and gardening formed the last part of Froebel's method.

Froebel's method advocated learning through play. The children had to 'do' something, as opposed to Pestalozzi's method of only observing 'objects'. This was a big step forward. But Froebel also remained imprisoned within the paradox created by himself and other, older enlightened educators. He wanted to give the children 'freedom' by subjecting them to a strict method, according to the 'laws of the nature of the child'. The practical result was often a routine orthodoxy. As an attempt to break through the mechanical teaching of young children, even Froebel's educational method did not free itself of this defect. To this day, 'Froebelen' is a Dutch term applied to childish routine behaviour in adults, like cutting out and gluing things together.

Women's science

Froebel was of the opinion that a good training was necessary in order to understand the deeper meaning of his method. In 1839 he started a training course for young men, but because of the lack of interest he soon admitted young women. Froebel's conviction that women, as they were more sensitive towards children than men were particularly suited to put his educational views into practice grew steadily: 'Women's love and children's love, children's life, child care and the female mind are one, according to their essence' (Froebel, 1922: 29). Upbringing should become 'the science of women' because 'women . . . realize what the spirit of man has inspired in them', wrote Froebel (Van Calcar, 1910).

Women had to remain subservient to his ideal. He wanted nothing to do with the emancipation of women. He showed himself to be extremely shocked by the 'Hochschule für Frauen' (Women's college), which was established in 1850, and where, amongst other things, women were trained to be kindergarten teachers (Taylor-Allen, 1982). The leadership was almost entirely in the hands of women. The teaching plan consisted not only of practical knowledge about early education, but also academic courses in literature, foreign languages, geography, mathematics, chemistry, religious history and pedagogy. Originally, Froebel was closely involved with the Hochschule, but he wanted nothing to do with the way in which young women used the education to gain personal and economic independence (Mueller, 1928). But this Hochschule showed that women could use Froebel's theories for their own ends.

WOMEN AND THE KINDERGARTEN MOVEMENT

It was only after Froebel's death in 1852 that the kindergarten idea become a success, thanks to the efforts of women from the upper classes and the aristocracy. For instance, the German Baroness Bertha von Marenholtz-Bülow became famous for her propaganda trips for the movement in Germany, Britain, the Netherlands, Belgium, France, Switzerland and Italy (Mueller, 1928). Her books about Froebel were translated into English and became famous in the United States. In the 'Fröbelstiftung' (Froebel Foundation), established by her, Froebelian teachers from all over the world were trained. Many advocates of the kindergarten movement in many different countries, such as Elise van Calcar in the Netherlands, Charles Dickens in England and Elizabeth Palmer Peabody in the United States, came into contact with Froebel's ideas through Bertha von Marenholtz.

In her propaganda, the Baroness conveniently made use of the fear, prevalent amongst the rich, of 'the red danger', and the rebelliousness and immorality in the working classes. In this she was no different from the advocates of the 'infant school' forty years earlier. Von Marenholtz advocated special 'philanthropic kindergartens', where well-trained women from the upper and middle classes could take care of the upbringing of working-class children.

Von Marenholtz called upon women from the upper classes to bring about a regeneration of the divided and demoralized world. She opposed political and societal rights for women. According to her, woman's power and influence lay in *her original right: her right as mother and educator.* She was, however, in favour of further education for girls, in order to enable them to develop their pedagogic talents.

In contrast to Bertha von Marenholtz, two other supporters of the Froebel movement in Germany, Johanna Goldschmidt and Henriette Goldschmidt, were active in the German women's movement (Mueller, 1928; Taylor-Allen, 1982). Both women founded a Hochschule für Frauen, for education in pedagogic science for the sex 'that is predestined to build the future'. They strove for women's right to an intellectual development, economic independence and civil rights.

A fourth Froebel supporter was his niece Henriette Schrader-Breymann, who was friendly with famous German feminists of the time. She herself became famous for the Pestalozzi-Fröbelhaus, which she founded with her husband in 1880 in Berlin (Philippi-Siewertsz van Reesema, 1949; Mueller, 1928). She offered practical help and pedagogic support to working-class mothers and children. There was day-care for the babies and infants of working mothers. For elementary school children there was after-school care. For mothers, there were mother's meetings, and courses on cookery, housekeeping and child-care. Henriette Schrader wanted to support mothers in their task of bringing up children, unlike Bertha von Marenholtz, who wanted to take it over entirely.

Henriette Schrader liberated Froebel's methods from their symbolism and rigidity. She endeavoured to create a family atmosphere by cooking, cleaning, tidying up and gardening with the children. From a very early age the children were given their own particular task and their own responsibility for carrying it out. The Pestalozzi-Fröbelhaus became internationally renowned, and one of the regular guests was Stanley Hall, later the leader of the American Child Study Movement. Through Stanley Hall and other Americans, the Pestalozzi-Fröbelhaus influenced innovations in American infant education and the Child Study Movement. (see the next chapter).

SPIRITUAL MOTHERHOOD

The most important women in the German Froebel movement came from a liberal background, where it was believed that education was the way to progress, freedom and a universal culture (Taylor-Allen, 1982). As women from the upper and middle classes, they found themselves increasingly excluded from professional work by the separation of work and family. There was barely any further education for girls during the first half of the nineteenth century, and women were economically dependent on their families or husbands. In spite of this, these women resisted having their lives restricted to the household in their own way, and longed for more responsibility.

With their male counterparts, these women shared their resistance to the 'despotism and obscurantism' of traditional society. They believed in the possibility of elevating society through education. In addition, they saw their chance to use the 'mothering instinct' to their own advantage. As child raisers they could play their own 'feminine' part – inside and outside the family – in the 'moral regeneration of humanity'.

Influential enlightened pedagogues such as Locke and Rousseau, were, in essence, patriarchal. Locke's pedagogic treatise consisted of letters from a father about his son's upbringing. Reason and rationality were the most important ingredients of upbringing as far as Locke was concerned. Mothers, emotionality, tenderness and loving care remained almost unmentioned in Rousseau's *Emile*. The mother, although indispensable for the natural development of the child, was reduced to being a 'wet-nurse'. The father or governor was actual educator. 'Feminine', emotional involvement with children was very often seen as a threat to enlightened, rational (male) upbringing.

Seen in this context, it is perhaps understandable that women sought support from the pedagogues who valued traditional, maternal love and care, in fact even placed more value on it than on the 'male' rationality.

Comenius and Pestalozzi were the first to value thoughtful, rational maternal love, before Froebel, but Froebel did more. He developed a method entwined with a mystic philosophical thesis, and laid the basis for a 'women's science'. He showed how mothers could make the most important elements in human life tangible for their babies, by playing 'galloping horses' and 'clapping hands', seemingly trivial things left unmentioned by many of his predecessors.

Whereas modern feminists never tire of protesting against the idea that only mothers are responsible for children's upbringing, nineteenth-century women welcomed the recognition of their influence on the psychological and physical well-being of their children. In the Netherlands, Elise van Calcar exulted in the 'powers of first impressions', which in her view would elevate the value placed on mothers and on all women by society. Froebel's conviction that the female sex had to be saved from its passive and instinctive situation, and was in need of a 'women's science', was welcomed by women (Taylor-Allen, 1982). His statement on women's mission, to save humanity with their female contribution, was one of the texts most often quoted by his female supporters.

Women outside the Froebel movement gave force to their demands by pointing out the special female talents that would have a good influence on the family and society as a whole. *The doctrine of spiritual motherhood*, as Taylor-Allen (1982) calls it, originated, according to her, in women's struggle for autonomy in the nineteenth century. Within this feminist stream, the complementary character of the female role was emphasized as one which needed more equal valuation.

The kindergarten movement offered women the possibility of further education, a professional perspective, status and an income. Froebel's philosophy gave a point of departure for the study of children and a philosophy for their education. Although often very obscure, his philosophical reflections referred to questions of good and evil, of the Divine in man, of the relationship between the generations, of being a woman or a man – a human being – and also of the Utopian society in which men and women would live together as equals.

The women within the kindergarten movement wrote books, gave lectures, founded kindergartens, and organized training courses on Froebelian pedagogics for girls and mothers. Their horizons were broadened beyond the boundaries of their own country. There was a great deal of travel and correspondence within Europe and between Europe and the United States, in order to exchange ideas. The kindergarten movement was truly an international movement.

THE KINDERGARTEN MOVEMENT AS AN INTERNATIONAL PHENOMENON

In Germany there was a great deal of resistance to the Froebel movement. In a number of towns the founding of a kindergarten was opposed by Church authorities, who were afraid of the effect of the competition on their own infant schools (Taylor-Allen, 1982). Well-to-do citizens preferred a governess or nanny in the family, rather than having their children educated in groups in a kindergarten. The kindergarten teachers were often so badly paid that there was no question of economic independence. The profession of kindergarten teacher did not offer the prospects of development and economic independence originally hoped for by the leading feminists.

In 1914, only 5 per cent of all German children attended a kindergarten or conventional infant school. In spite of the attempts by Froebel's supporters to make child-care a science, *Infant education and motherhood remained non-paid or un(der)paid and undervalued women's work.*

However, the influence of the German kindergarten supporters was not limited to their own country. Von Marenholtz's journeys have already been mentioned, but besides this, the emigration of fervent supporters of kindergartens to the United States, Britain and other European countries also played a role. To a large extent these emigrants were women who, together with their husbands, were forced to leave Germany because of the conservative political climate after the revolutionary tensions in 1848. In 1854 the first kindergarten in Britain was founded by

German immigrants/refugees, and in the United States in 1855. In various countries in Europe and in the United States, a kindergarten movement developed. I will sketch the development of the kindergarten movement in the following section, in order to point out the similarities and differences between the Froebel movements in these countries. In addition, I will outline the American situation is added as background information for the child study movement, that started towards the end of the nineteenth century (see the next chapter).

THE NETHERLANDS: THE FROEBEL SCHOOL

Round about 1850 there were a number of different sorts of schools for young children in the Netherlands. Most of them were not registered, and there was no national law or control governing them. It is most likely that the level of hygiene, pedagogy and teaching was extremely low. Coronel (1864) described them as 'live piles of manure' and 'child warehouses', where children 'recite psalms, learn texts by heart, repeat rhymes, scream out songs and spell out words'.

Froebel went a step further, compared to Pestalozzi and his object lessons. Froebel took the child's need for activity and play into account, but even Pestalozzi's method was not practised everywhere.

Froebel's ideas gained ground only slowly in the Netherlands, and remained limited mainly to the methodic and didactic area. After 1870, most textbooks included detailed instructions on how to use the 'gifts' and the 'occupations' step by step. Froebel schools developed, but the original idea of working and playing in gardens found no response. 'The concept of garden was lost in the concept of *the school*' (Van Calcar, 1898). Froebel's philosophic and pedagogic writings were not translated into Dutch until 1922. In 1929, 82.8 per cent of all infant schools in the Netherlands said they used the Froebel method, but we should not read too much into this. Until the beginning of the twentieth century, reports were still being made of too many children in one classroom, insufficient teaching material and a mechanical application of the Froebel method (Singer, 1989: 128).

'Women's science' did not materialize in the Netherlands either, even though Elise van Calcar, following the German example, founded a training school for girls from the better classes, in order to prepare them for their task as infant te and mothers. But the initiative was not followed by others. 1 ever, training courses for Froebel teachers were developed, ␣ut without the feminist ideal of the moral elevation of society.

In the Netherlands the Froebel method contributed to the rise in the status of infant schools, as a pedagogically acceptable form of preparatory education. But this rise in status went hand in hand with a further discrediting of the 'care' function of these schools (Clerkx, 1984). Taking care of the children of working mothers was not one of the Dutch Froebel schools' tasks. Besides, because of the emphasis on methods, the difference between methodical and rational upbringing on the one hand, and ordinary upbringing and care on the other, was highlighted. Mothers were supposedly falling short on the methodical side. A good mother was to leave part of the upbringing to a qualified teacher, but, at the same time, she was also expected to remain available at home. What once started as a method for mothers, designed by Froebel on the basis of his (idealized) view of how mothers bring up children at home, became a Froebel school, where the pedagogic inability and inexperience of the mothers was emphasized.

BRITAIN: LOWER-CLASS INFANT SCHOOLS AND MIDDLE-CLASS KINDERGARTENS

In Britain Froebel's ideas met with much more enthusiasm, especially amongst the middle class. In Britain, Bertha von Marenholtz-Bülow's lectures generated a great deal of interest. Froebel's romantic ideas corresponded to the work of the romantic authors such as Wordsworth, Dickens, Eliot and Charlotte Brontë, in which the pure, spontaneous and emotional child was contrasted with an immoral, rationalistic, loveless and selfish society (Rusk, 1933; Whitbread, 1972; Woodham-Smith, 1952). Elementary education inspectors were also interested in kindergartens. In Britain, infant schools were already a recognized part of national education, but, just as in the Netherlands, there was a great deal of anxiety about the boring character of this preparatory education. It was felt that the quality of infant schools could be raised by using Froebel's methods.

English Froebel literature was soon published, including the first translations of Froebel's philosophic-pedagogic work.

Round about 1855, conditions seemed favourable for a new wave of pedagogic innovations, but this did not materialize. The steps taken in order to lower the rising cost of national education were disastrous for the quality of education for young children. There was also resistance to Froebel's learning through play. According to an observer of the time, there were two rival theories:

> One party said 'take time by the forelock, teach infants their prescribed tasks before they are legally required to repeat them; by mere reiteration the tasks will become familiar'; the other party said 'develop the infant's powers; teach him to attend, to construct, and "change" the standards'.
>
> (Quoted in Woodham-Smith, 1952: 57)

But in the end it was the unwillingness to spend money on young children from the working class which decided the matter. A kindergarten required smaller classes, well-trained teachers and sufficient toys and play material. Another reason was that this freer form of education was thought to be less suitable for children from the lower social classes.

Froebel's philosophy on education was better suited to the possibilities and philosophy of the enlightened English middle class. Campaigns for education for girls were successfully coupled to Froebel's philosophy that infant education was a science (Marks,1976; Pederson, 1972; Woodham-Smith, 1952). Most of the schools belonging to the Girls' Public Day School Trust, founded in 1873, included a kindergarten for the necessary practical experience. Training courses for kindergarten teachers were founded for middle-class girls; these made high demands on their intellectual abilities. Besides this, shorter training courses were developed for girls from less well-off families, to train them as Froebel child-minders.

From the start, the British kindergarten movement was very aware that it was part of an *international movement*. Many German women were recruited for work in English kindergartens; there was a great deal of travel and correspondence. After 1880, when the kindergarten movement in the United States became stronger, the American influence also grew.

Although the number of kindergartens in Britain remained few, their influence on thought about the upbringing of young children was probably large. Through informative literature, the Froebel gifts and occupations found their way into middle-class families. In 1895, Froebelians founded the Sesame Club, in order to interest parents in new methods of upbringing. In the light of the new philosophy on education, and the practice in kindergartens, the poor quality of baby classes and infant schools became more apparent. However, very few charitable kindergartens were founded: at the end of the nineteenth century there were only four (Whitbread, 1972, 45).

During the entire second half of the nineteenth century, the number of children under the age of 5 within the national education system grew, but dame schools also continued to play a large part (Leinster-Mackay, 1976).

The rise in the number of children attending school up to 1900 cannot be explained by the needs of working mothers; this increase until 1900 coincided with a decrease in the number of mothers in employment. From a survey carried out in 1908, it appeared that parents sent their children to school because there it was warm, clean and safe, the children learned good manners and obedience, and mothers could work (Tizard, Moss and Perry, 1976: 61–3).

After 1900 there was a marked decline in the numbers. Indirectly, this was probably partly due to Froebel's influence on the changing pedagogic ideas in the middle class, making the mother's role more important. The education offered to young children fell into disrepute. The reasons for this were the catastrophic defeats in the Boer War, and the soldiers' poor general health (Davin, 1983). The poor health of the soldiers was

Table 4.1 Number and percentage of 3- and 4-year-olds in schools in Britain, 1870–1 to 1930–1[1]

	Children at school	All children	%
1870–71	275,608	1,179,228	24.2
1880–81	393,056	1,339,826	29.3
1890–91	458,267	1,377,818	33.2
1900–1	615,607	1,428,597	43.1
1910–11	350,591	1,540,542	22.7
1920–21	175,467	1,147,685	15.3
1930–31	159,335	1,213,000	13.1

[1] 2-year-olds were not registered

associated with mothers working outside the home in the working classes.

The example was given of 2-year-olds already attending a school, whose bodies and minds were being ruined by boring tasks and sitting still all day long. Female educational inspectors proposed the organization of special facilities for very young children: 'nursery schools'. But there was no money available for this. Further cuts in the national education system led to the exclusion of young children.

Thus there came an end to a long period in which education for young children from the working classes had been taken for granted. From the beginning of the twentieth century the interventions in the upbringing of young children (to start with, mainly medically orientated), were aimed specifically at improving situations within the family. Mothers were given more advice and control over upbringing at home, instead of having the children placed outside the home (Lewis, 1980).

The United States: the crusade for kindergartens

For a short time round about 1820, infant schools imported from Europe were popular in the United States, but these had either disappeared or been included in the national education system by 1840. A greater value was placed on family upbringing for young children (Pence, 1986; Cavallo, 1979). In the same period, from 1820, mothers' associations sprang up everywhere (Cott, 1977; Sunley, 1955; Wishy, 1968). Mothers' associations in New England – where most research has been carried out – were usually connected to the Church, and were part of a network of women's groups, such as women's prayer groups, Sunday school work, charity work and missionary work. In her book *The Bonds of Womanhood* (1977), Nancy Cott describes how the idealization of womanhood developed in the United States. The 'women's sphere' and the 'cult of true womanhood' found its roots in the network of women's organizations. In mothers' groups women talked about literature on raising children and education. 'Breaking the will' and 'conversion of children' were important subjects for discussion. Along with the recognition of the importance of the first years of childhood, the status of mothers in the United States grew. Motherhood was elevated to a profession that had to be learnt.

During the first half of the nineteenth century, only a small group of innovation-minded pedagogues and doctors were interested in the enlightened theories on upbringing, such as those of Rousseau and Pestalozzi (Wishy, 1968; Shapiro, 1985: 1–18). For instance, in 1839, the pedagogic experiment run by Alcott in a Boston infant school had to be stopped, even though he was called 'the American Pestalozzi'. Conversations about the birth of Jesus Christ and human reproduction went too far for the Christian community.

Within this American context, it is hardly surprising that the first kindergarten, founded by German refugees in 1855, received little interest. Only one or two took note, like Elizabeth Palmer Peabody, one of Alcott's former colleagues, who was so impressed that she organized a study trip to Europe in order to find out more about the kindergarten movement there. It was only in 1880 that kindergartens became a success, and their numbers grew rapidly from 400 in 1880 to 2,884 in 1898 (Vandewalker, 1908: 23). From this time on, in the United States the kindergarten movement became more influential than in many European countries.

To what did they owe this success? According to Wishy (1968), before 1860 in the United States the child was seen to be redeemable if given a good upbringing; only later is it seen to be the bearer of a better future, a redeemer. This new way of thinking was very apparent amongst the intellectuals who held important positions in the national education system. Froebel's philosophy coincided with this, besides which, many key figures in the national education system saw, as in Europe, the importance of preparatory education (Weber, 1969: 27–36).

A second background is the American tradition of women's organizations. Froebel's ideas on women's educative mission concurred with older notions on the moral superiority of women. The most famous Froebel teachers were the deeply religious women, who became interested in kindergartens through their work in Sunday schools and their fight against alcohol (Snyder, 1972). A few were also active suffragettes, fighters for women's right to vote.

Women carried the kindergarten movement. They were the ones to collect money for kindergartens; they, as the wives and daughters of millionaires, gave money; they earned money by becoming Froebel teachers; they worked as voluntary workers in the kindergartens; they developed themselves intellectually, socially and politically with the 'kindergarten crusade' (Feinstein, 1980). Just as for European women, the kindergarten movement offered one of the few opportunities to study, for a personal income and socially acceptable work outside the family. Even in elementary education, where a relatively large number of women worked, they were excluded from any managerial positions. The kindergartens became their own territory, where women called the tune. Prominent Froebel teachers were even convinced of an educative mission as far as elementary education was concerned. They were responsible for the introduction of subjects such as drawing, playing and music in elementary education. According to Vandewalker (1908), between 1870 and 1880 more books were published about kindergartens than all other books on up-bringing and education put together.

A third influential factor on the success of the kindergarten movement in America was the toy industry. In the United States this industry was quick to see the possibilities of this new need and marketing area. Through mass production Froebel's gifts could be brought on to the market cheaply. In advertising campaigns their educative value was highly praised, which led to every middle-class family possessing some sort of Froebel toy (Shapiro, 1985: 69–73).

A fourth factor in this success is probably the stream of new groups of immigrants from eastern and southern Europe during the eighties. These immigrants had different habits and traditions, and languages totally incomprehensible to the mainly English-speaking American population. The enormous numbers of newcomers settling in the slums of the industrial cities caused the 'old' Americans a great deal of anxiety. Various new forms of philanthropy developed, aimed at preventive intervention and the education of the population. Charitable or free kindergartens fitted into this policy of preventive intervention. Kindergarten teachers were seen as replacements for the mother who drank and led a life of debauchery, or simply worked. The process of Americanization of the young immigrants had to start before the parents and the neighbourhood had a chance to corrupt the innocent child:

You cannot catch your citizen too early in order to make him a good citizen. The kindergarten age marks our earliest opportunity to catch the little Russian, the little German, Pole, Syrian, and the rest and begin to make good American Citizens of them. And our little American-born citizen is often in quite as much need of early catching and training.

(Quoted in Lazerson, 1972)

Community work and the education of mothers through home visiting were an integral part of the work in the free kindergartens (Ross, 1976). In the various states the number of children attending a kindergarten differed enormously: in 1912 in five states, less than 1 per cent of all 4- and 5-year-olds attended a kindergarten, whilst in other states, such as New York and New Jersey, 20 to 30 per cent of this age group attended a kindergarten (Ross, 1976: 90).

From 1890, the free kindergartens were absorbed more and more by the public national education system. This meant a recognition of their educative value, but also the loss of their character as a form of charitable work: voluntary workers were replaced by paid teachers; home visitation, the education of mothers and community work were, to a great extent, lost; the groups became larger and school hours were adapted; children under 4 years old were excluded; the education became more academic and aimed more at preparation for elementary education. Above all, women lost their managerial positions. As school heads and theoreticians they had to make way for men. Women's main role became that of assistants (Shapiro, 1985: 131–50).

MOTHERHOOD: IDEALIZED AND LIBELLED

At the start of this chapter I posed the question why nineteenth century women sought their emancipation in motherhood. This question was partly occasioned by present-day feminist discussions, in which motherhood is seen as an obstacle to emancipation. What are the differences and the similarities between these apparently contradictory feminist standpoints? As far as I can see, the key to the answer to this question must lie in the different feminist reactions to *the separation of the world of the family from the world of paid employment*. The nineteenth-century Froebelians attempted to obtain a position outside the family by gaining professional recognition and valuation of the 'feminine' qualities in children's upbringing. They strove for their 'original right of motherhood', and defended the rights of 'the child'. The kindergarten was an instrument for the Froebelians in the feminist struggle to better the position of women and children. Through this they wished to elevate humanity.

Second-wave feminists also tried to break through the separation of paid employment and family. They wanted paid employment to be combinable with the care of children. Contrary to the first-wave feminists, they resisted the idea that, biologically, women are supposed to be 'feminine' and 'motherly'. They wanted child centres in the mothers' interest.

At first sight, the first-wave feminists' attitude towards motherhood would seem to be contradictory to that of the second-wave feminists. However, these two feminist attitudes to motherhood are not totally contradictory. The Froebelians and the present-day feminists strove, and still strive, for an improvement in the position of women, and both feminist movements have in common their encounter with the lack of value attributed to bringing up children. The Froebelians were forced to discover that in the end the education of young children remained undervalued and un(der)paid women's work. The 'male' forms of education turned out to be more powerful than their 'feminine' methods. Present-day feminists are galled to discover that the emancipation of one group of women is partly based on the un(der)paid work done by another group of women.

The present struggle for child-care is often seen as women's right to work outside the home. But with just as much right, the struggle for child-care for the children of working mothers can be seen as a struggle for a financial reward for bringing up young children! Good and loving care for children outside the home makes the cost of this in terms of the work time and effort of those responsible, more visible. Perhaps the characterization of this by the Dutch doctor Catharina van Tusschenbroek in 1898 is still applicable: 'motherhood, idealized in words and libelled in deeds'.

Chapter 5

Laboratories of human relationships

The rise of a scientific pedagogy in the United States, and the role of the nursery schools in this process (1890–1940)

Progress beyond other plans for early education is sought in the following ways: 1. By applying as far as possible in nursery school practice all available scientific knowledge; 2. by providing as far as possible the advice of specialists and the continuous expert guidance of the growth process; 3. by observation and experiment under controlled conditions in the effort to obtain more knowledge about the preschool child, a deeper insight into his needs, and consequently a finer control of the growth process during the years of early childhood.

(Ilse Forest, 1929)

CHILD STUDIES AND HOW CHILD REARING BECAME MORE SCIENTIFIC

In 1895, during a summer course given at the Clarke University in Massachusetts, Dr G. Stanley Hall tried to convince thirty-five prominent American kindergarten teachers of the importance of his child studies. Hall argued that child rearing should be based on empirical research into child behaviour, and not on metaphysical contemplations, as in Froebel's case. According to Hall, new scientific facts challenged Froebel's playing method. Thirty-five offended kindergarten teachers stood up and left. However, two women stayed behind, Anna Bryan and Patty Hill (Snyder, 1972: 178; Ross, 1976: 71). Both women were to play a large part in the more scientific approach to education in kindergartens.

The clash in 1895 was just one moment in a struggle that was to continue until 1925, leaving the supporters of the new child psychology as the uncontested winners. At a practical level, this struggle was about raffia plaiting, cutting-out and pasting as prescribed by Froebel, as opposed to free play (Hall) or the making of useful articles such as a mat for the doll's house (Dewey). But, behind this was a complete revolution in philosophy about children, upbringing and the founding of moral order. Instead of metaphysics, religious introspection and the penetration of the intrinsic logic of things through intuition, *faith in scientific observations* was born.

In America in the 1890s and 1920s two child-study movements were started. Their prime aim was to make upbringing more scientific. People involved in upbringing were to follow children's 'natural development' according to scientific theories and research (Hall; Gesell), and/or by the applying theories on natural laws (Thorndike, Watson).

Both child-study movements signified a break away from the pedagogic philosophy of the period leading up to the twentieth century. The move away from metaphysics and the hunger for facts were new ideas. Large groups of children were researched in order to discover average growth curves and the natural laws involved. However, there was also a certain continuity. American research at the end of the nineteenth century expanded further on the baby diaries, such as those by Preyer (1882), and on child studies carried out by the educators Pestalozzi, Froebel, Alcott and many others. Twentieth-century child psychologists also made moral statements. 'Healthy' and 'normal' development became scientifically founded aims with a general validity. 'Deviations from the norm' had to be corrected, and tests were developed in order to do this.

This chapter gives a description of both child-study movements. I will pay special attention to the rift that was created between the 'objective' scientific knowledge and the knowledge of parents/mothers as non-experts; this lay knowledge was supposedly of less value, leaving all parents/mothers apparently in need of scientific assistance. Apart from this, I will also consider the connection which developed between the 'child-orientated' upbringing in special 'children's spaces' (kindergartens and nursery schools), on the one hand, and, on the other, the need of parents/teachers for more information about normal development of children. In order to be able to follow this natural development, it had to be measurable: is this child developing normally or does he/she need some correction? Developmental psychologists set down aims for child-orientated pedagogic methods by describing normal, healthy development. Thus a child-orientated pedagogy and the concept of 'natural development' were introduced.

THE CHILD-STUDY MOVEMENT IN THE 1890s

'The contents of children's minds'

In 1883, G. Stanley Hall shocked parents and teachers with the publication of his research into the 'contents of children's minds'. According to Hall, there was a great lack of general knowledge amongst 4- to 8-year-olds; they did not understand everyday concepts such as 'beehive', 'rib' or 'pine tree'. Hall was not just anybody; he was, after all, the first psychologist with a university degree in the United States, and therefore he spoke with authority as a man of science.

'The contents of children's minds' was a quantitative survey into children's knowledge of a large number of concepts such as ant, pig, potatoes, buttercups, hips, ankles, sunrise, island, woods, more, less. There were a large number of terms from, country life which mirrored the romantic view of children apparent in kindergarten education at the time. The aim of this research was to describe children's knowledge and way of thinking, in order to formulate pedagogic rules. *How did Hall make this step from descriptive facts to prescriptive conclusions?*

In the first place Hall established that a large number of children did not know the concepts that were supposed to be known at elementary school level. Country children knew more than city children; and children who had attended a kindergarten knew more than those who had not. His first prescriptive conclusions were based on these facts. He advised parents to acquaint their children with country life, or send them to a kindergarten. He advised teachers to research the knowledge of the children in their class carefully, exactly, and bit by bit,in order to prevent them being filled with words of which they had no understanding (Hall, 1921: 23–5). Even now, this sort of recommendation is not unusual as a form of evaluation research into the way the school connects to the starting level of the children.

However, Hall goes further and takes a second step, shifting from 'this is the way it is' to 'this is the way it should be'. He had presumably shown that country life had more pedagogic value for the *natural development* of the child than city life. In order to substantiate this he did not refer to Froebel, but introduced his own *recapitulation theory*. This theory maintains that during its development (ontogenesis) the child repeats the evolution of the species (philogenesis). According to Hall, the answers given by the children revealed their primitive way of thinking, something they have in common with primitive races and 'wild tribes'. For instance, children thought that stars were lights lit by God; that thunderstorms were caused by God hitting the clouds; that the earth was as round and flat as a dollar piece (Hall, 1921: 32–5). Hall was convinced that in order to undergo a healthy development, children must be given the opportunity to work through all the various stages that correspond to the development of mankind. In his famous essay in 1901, 'The Ideal School as Based on Child Study' (Hall, 1974), he developed this idea further, stating that the kindergarten formed a foundation for an ideal education system. During the phase of poetic fantasy and mythical thinking, children should be given the space to play freely in order to vent their primitive instincts. Physical and emotional development he supposed to be more important than intellectual development. However, children between the ages of 8 and 12 were more in need of discipline and authority. At this stage, drilling, habit forming, and reading and writing lessons were seen to be good and natural.

The very youngest children belonged at home with their mother. According to his recapitulation theory, women were closer to young children than men. The woman's larger, lower brain centre made her suited to producing milk, bearing children, and loving and caring for them. Hall warned of the danger of intellectual development, as this damaged a woman's reproductive ability, made her less fertile, and resulted in weaker children. Were women inferior to men? Hall would have hastened to deny this. 'The glorified madonna ideal shows us how much more whole and holy it is to be a woman than to be an artist, orator, professor, or expert' (cited in Diehl, 1986: 870).

Hall combined religious and scientific principles to form a whole, and scientific statements merged with political, social and pedagogic rules. On the one hand, Hall endeavoured to free his thinking of metaphysical speculation and to base it on empirical research into children, but on the other hand, he remained confined to idealistic notions of 'nature', 'growth' and the mother as 'madonna'. According to Hall's biographer, Dorothy Ross (1972), at the end of the nineteenth century, people like Hall took social structures and moral values for granted to such an extent that natural, religious and social laws seemed to combine to be one and the same thing. Other historians, such as Siegel and White (1982) and Cavallo (1979), propose quite the opposite: precisely because the social structures and moral values had become so uncertain, Hall and his followers felt the need for a new set of morals not based on religion, but seemingly neutral moral standards based on objective empirical research into 'natural development'.

Hall and the child-study movement: success and criticism

After 'The Contents of Children's Minds', Hall received repeated requests for more child studies. However, Hall devoted himself to experimental psychology. It was to be another eight years before he took up his interest in child studies, driven partly by financial problems. As president of the Clark University, Hall was struggling with financial and organizational problems. The university needed financial backing, and wider public interest in the results of scientific research (Ross, 1972: 279).

In 1891 Hall started giving lectures to teachers, and he founded a new magazine, *Pedagogical Seminary*. At that time he was not doing any scientific research, but he did have a vision of the future: by coordinating the practice of upbringing with the child's nature, as established in the child studies, he hoped to produce healthy children (Siegel and White, 1982: 256–9). In order to learn more about the child's nature, Hall and his assistants developed a large number of questionnaires on a wide range of subjects: child humour; food (likes and dislikes); children's self-image; children's collections; reactions to light and darkness; withdrawal; fears; dreams; memories; anger; jealousy; dolls; movement ability; toys; cloud and moon fantasies; moral and religious feelings; and so on. The questionnaires were filled in by trained research assistants, and later by thousands of upper- and middle-class parents, especially mothers, and by teachers, on the basis of observations, experience or prejudices, although very often the basis was not even clear.

Carrying out child studies became very popular (Schlossman, 1976), and tens of thousands of completed questionnaires were sent to Hall, and were, where possible, processed and interpreted by him in the light of his recapitulation theory. As time went on, the care Hall had originally taken with the validity and reliability of his research gradually disappeared. His recapitulation theory remained global and vague – a fact, however, which did not prevent Hall from giving 'scientific' pedagogic advice with great conviction.

Why were Hall's child studies such a success? During the last decade of the nineteenth century in the United States, the consequences of a gradual change from a mainly agricultural, colonial society, to a more town-orientated, capitalistic society were being felt (Grubb and Lazerson, 1982). Upbringing had to become more open because of social mobility and rapidly changing societal circumstances. The conveyance of knowledge previously taken for granted disappeared, and in some cases was actively opposed, as in the case of immigrant children. This formed the basis for an enormous interest in advice on upbringing shown by parents and teachers alike.

The end of the nineteenth century was also the period in which a number of new institutions and facilities for children were introduced: clinics for babies; homes for handicapped children; homes and foster parents for abandoned, maltreated and neglected children; and (reformatory) approved schools (Platt, 1977; Levine and Levine, 1970; Siegel and White, 1982). These new institutions still had to develop ways and methods of working, and were very much in need of information about the children in their care. Because of the new compulsory education systems introduced in a number of states, whole groups of children started going to school. The stream of non-English-speaking immigrant children meant that the approach to children at school needed reassessment.

There were a number and variety of reforms in upbringing at the end of the nineteenth century, often known as the 'progressive education movement', its most important advocates being people like John Dewey and Jane Addams. A great belief in the possibilities of creating a democratic society through education, upbringing and science, formed a part of this progressivism. Research into the living conditions of people, and their problems and needs, was very important for making policies.Teaching methods were to be based on psychological and sociological insights (Cremin, 1962).

The above-mentioned developments also affected the up-bringing of young children. In particular, the so-called 'free kindergartens' with their many immigrant children and their orthodox Froebel methods emphasizing religious symbols, were put under pressure (Shapiro, 1985: 85–130). For instance, Kate Douglas Smith described how she had to work in the back streets of San Francisco. 'Many days were spent in learning the unpronouncable names of my flock and in keeping them from murdering one another until Froebel's justly celebrated "law of love" could be made a working proposition' (cited in Weber, 1969: 43).

Kate Douglas Smith, Anna Bryan, Patty Hill and other kinder-garten teachers started, out of pure necessity, to experiment with new work methods. They sought contact with Hall and his followers. But Hall's biggest success did not lie with the Froebelians – where there was also much opposition – but amongst the upper-middle-class mothers, often with a university education, who had both the time and the intelligence to devote themselves to 'the cause' (Schlossman, 1976).

In 1892, the American Association of University Women formed a study group on child studies. All over the country study groups emerged, where Hall's questionnaires were filled in and discussions held on the new scientific insights, and their rele-vance to their own children. Apart from this, these women tried to introduce new ideas into the education system and amongst the poorer mothers. In 1897, the first National Congress of Mothers was held, with G. Stanley Hall as the main speaker. In 1915 the National Congress of Mothers became the first national organization for parent education with its own magazine, its own congresses and study groups, an eight-volume encyclopaedia with information about children, and 60,000 paying members.

In the nineties, the child-study movement was likewise a parent education movement. The movement was also coupled with feminism, and, once again, we see that upper- and middle-class women try to give some sort of form to their feminism by making sure that their own education benefits their children as well as the education of the lower social classes. Hall's glorifica-tion of the mother appealed particularly to this group of women.

However, there was also strong criticism of Hall's child-study movement, first by orthodox Froebelians, and secondly by scien-tists who wanted to rid psychology of its amateurism, such as the collecting of data by laymen. According to the orthodox, child studies offered nothing but an inventory of facts about the mind, without contributing to a better understanding of the higher forms of love and rationality. The latter could only be achieved by introspection, based on religion and philosophy. Hall's ideas about the importance of free play for young children were seen as heretical. What had happened to the feeling of unity that the child could only experience through maternal love and Froebel's play symbols (Shapiro, 1985: 107–29; Weber, 1969: 47–64)?

As for the scientists, they accused Hall of too much idealism and too little science. The collection of data by laymen meant that the demands of scientific objectivity were not met. Reliability, systemics and validity were supposedly below standard (Bradbury, 1937; Schlossman, 1976, 1981).

After 1900, the popularity of the child-study movement went into decline. Hall remained popular with parents and teachers, but for scientists it became suspect to have anything to do with him; in these circles, filling in questionnaires was seen as a pleasant way for women to pass the time. In retrospect, it was probably the latter that was the most important to Hall's child-study movement. Hall made the general public more aware of the possibilities of a more detached, observant attitude towards children, and awakened an interest in science. According to Schlossman (1976), filling in questionnaires possibly served as 'sensitivity training'. Through Hall, the connection between the university, parents and teachers was established.

DEWEY AND THORNDIKE

In the world of kindergartens, the period between 1890 and 1925 was one of confusion, ideaological conflicts and experiments with teaching plans (Cavallo, 1976, 1979; Shapiro, 1983: 107–30; Weber, 1969: 65–97). The orthodox Froebelians did not only have Hall and his followers to deal with. Within the progressive educational movement more theories existed about child development as well as views on the relationship between science and pedagogic practice. Concerning this, Dewey and Thorndike were very important, and to a lesser extent Montessori, whose work found little recognition in the United States. Freud's influence remained confined to a few experimental kindergartens for the children of artists and intellectuals (Steere, 1968; Sulman, 1973; Hale, 1971).

Dewey (1859–1952) was a professor of philosophy with a great interest in psychology and education. In 1899 he wrote *School and Society*, a book referred to as *the* pedagogic credo of the progressive movement at the turn of the century (Cremin, 1962: 117–19). One of Dewey's main points was that society brings up its children. In earlier agricultural communities, children learned by working with adults, and the entire process of production in the household and at work was directly accessible to children. According to him, industrialization led to the loss of this direct form of learning. He also felt that Froebel's methods were too formal and rigid, and were too irrelevant to the child's daily life (Dewey and Dewey, 1915: 111–27).

The school had to try to form a miniature society, where children could be confronted with situations (namely, problems, work and play) whose complexity reflected modern society. By working together to achieve a communal goal in a peer group, children would learn to subordinate *their* wishes and impulses to the will to collaborate. Dewey rejected Hall's idea of 'natural' laws of development; according to him this creates an abstract image of 'the child' which has nothing to do with real children. Of course education should start with psychological insight into the child's abilities, interests and habits, but these abilities, interests and habits should not be seen as something that is a part of the child, or something that a child 'possesses'; rather, they should be constantly interpreted within their social context, in terms of what children are able to do in relation to the people they live with.

Dewey's pragmatic philosophy contained a criticism of dualistic thought about individuals and society, body and mind, school and life. In his theoretical work, one of which was *Democracy and Education* (1916), he worked on these ideas. Apart from this, he was one of the first people to establish a 'laboratory school' at the university, in order to combine research and pedagogic practice. According to historians like Weber (1969) and Cavallo (1976), Dewey's scientific theories were too abstract for teachers to be able to put them into practice. His great influence, therefore, remained confined to slogans such as 'learning by doing'.

Dewey's theories also had little influence on developmental psychology and thought in universities (Siegel and White, 1982). The thirst for more knowledge regarding 'the child's' nature was apparently too great for Dewey's cultural relativity approach. Only recently has there been more interest in Dewey as a developmental psychologist (White, 1981).

Thorndike succeeded where Dewey had little success. He gained scientific acclaim and a following, and, at the same time, greatly influenced the practice of education. Thorndike (1874–1949), was a professor of psychology. In 1903 he published *Educational Psychology*, and a year later *Introduction to the Theory of Mental and Social Measurements*. In both books Thorndike tried to lay down the foundation for a natural scientific method of establishing laws of learning, and of measuring achievements and abilities. Whereas Hall wanted to give 'scientifically' founded values, standards and ideals, Thorndike presented himself more as a technician, giving the educators the instruments (tests/laws) with which to solve their problems. Thorndike depoliticized the relationship between psychology and pedagogic practice with his 'neutral' natural scientific psychology (Curti, 1961: 460–2).

According to Thorndike, humanity could improve itself by learning to adapt better to circumstances. Original instincts had to be transformed into socially acceptable habits by learning. Thorndike's view was that learning consisted of 'bonds of connection' between a situation (S) and a response (R). For some time he experimented with animals, and as a result of this he formulated three laws. The most important of these was the 'law of effect', 'the prime law of human control' (Thorndike, 1913: 227–8). According to this law, every response which meets with success in a given situation will be repeated, whilst a response resulting in an uncomfortable feeling will disappear. He was also convinced that learning should be measured exactly. He was a strong proponent of the introduction of tests in order to be able to monitor pupils achievements, and to 'analyse' the results of the education (Curti, 1961: 460).

During the first two decades of the twentieth century, habit training, along with the preparatory education, became one of the most important aims of the kindergarten and nursery school. Teaching methods for habit forming were reminiscent of Dewey, at least as far as the didactic form was concerned, but as far as the teaching aims were concerned, they were mainly influenced by Thorndike's thoughts on 'tests' and 'measurement'.

OBSERVATIONS, TESTS AND HABIT TRAINING

Why did teachers value Thorndike's tests and measurements so much? Perhaps Patty Smith Hill's developing philosophy can provide a key to the answer to this (Snyder, 1972: 256–70). Patty Smith Hill started studying with G. Stanley Hall as a kindergarten teacher. Later, she became fascinated by Dewey's work. She became a professor at Columbia University, and was given a kindergarten in order to carry out experiments, observations and research. In this kindergarten, inspired by Dewey, much space was given to creative activities and social life. There were building bricks for building houses and shops; also there were ladders, slides and swings, and smaller objects such as cars, dolls, pots and pans, and a shop with imitation money. Patty Smith Hill wanted to show scientifically the value of her kindergarten for social development, one of the reasons being to convince the general public. With the help of trained kindergarten teachers, the children were observed and their achievements classified in categories such as:

Ability to initiate purposes and plans
Ability to persevere or 'to stick to one's job' despite difficulties
Ability to lead and follow intelligently
Ability to work alone or in a group.
(Cited in Snyder, 1972: 263)

The results were published in *A Conduct Curriculum for the Kindergarten and First Grade* (1923). However, scientists found the list of 'abilities' too vague, they had to be operationalized in terms of behaviour. Thus, the 'Tentative Inventory of Habits' emerged: a list of eighty-four habits. Thorndike's authority as a scientist lent credibility to the inventory and it became very popular. It formed the basis for a detailed teaching plan for habit training. To illustrate this there follows the teaching plan for 4-year-olds: 'Washing hands before lunch":

Typical activities:

Washing hands
(individual pans, soap, paper towels)

Desirable changes in thought, feeling and conduct:

> to get pans quietly and without dropping them;
> to pour water from partly filled pitcher into pan and to carry without unnecessary splashing;
> to clean up after washing hands;
> pouring water into pail;
> wiping pan with paper towel;
> putting towel in scrap basket.

(Cited in Snyder, 1972: 263)

Such detailed 'habit programmes' had not been Patty Smith Hill's intention. She was worried that the observation diagrams were not functioning as a means of establishing the child's achievements during free play, but rather as aims that gave a rigid direction to education. Patty Smith Hill felt that *if only what is measurable counts, Dewey's original intentions would be lost.* However, Agnes Law Rogers, the psychologist responsible for the inventory, thought otherwise: 'The development of physical science meant the control of the material world and mental tests will ultimately mean control of human behaviour' (cited in Weber, 1969: 106).

Weber (1969), linked the popularity of tests, observation diagrams and habit training with the difficulties encountered by teachers when trying to place abstract principles such as 'following the natural development' (Hall), and 'learning by doing' (Dewey), into a concrete form or teaching plan. Knowledge of facts can be tested: the children either know something or they don't. But how does a teacher know if he or she is doing the right thing, if the child itself is the starting point as well as the goal? One solution to this problem is to have a clear picture of 'normal' development. Development had to be observable and measurable, in order to establish progress, and to give the professional educators something to go by. Nowadays, testing children is rarely seen as child-centred. But if we look back through history we can equally say that *child-centredness, and observations/tests/measuring all presuppose one another.* In connection with this, Walkerdine (1984) speaks of the 'psychology-pedagogy couple', a developmental psychology that gives the standards for pedagogic action, or, put a different way, a pedagogy that results in 'natural development'.

Around 1925, there was very little trace of the original Froebel methods, and the orthodox Froebelians had more or less vanished. Froebel's belief in the value of introspection and *maternal love/divine unity* had made way for the conviction that education should be based on observation, and that moral development takes place within the peer group through *habit training* (Cavallo, 1979).

THE CHILD STUDY MOVEMENT DURING THE 1920s AND 1930s

There was a second phase of child studies during the twenties and thirties. In 1917, the first Child Welfare Research Station was founded at the University of Iowa. This initiative was taken by a farmer's wife, Cora Bussey Hillis, who had lost two of her children through illness. *If research can improve the quality of pigs and grain, why can it not improve the quality of children?* she asked herself (Sears, 1975: 19). Ten years later there were eight large research centres in the United States, comparable to the one in Iowa. Furthermore, many universities had smaller research groups in the field of child studies. What was the cause of this sudden increase in child studies during the twenties?

The main reason is often said to have been the First World War (Sears, 1975; Senn, 1975; Cairns, 1983). Widespread conscription created the opportunity for mass medical and psychological testing. The results of the tests were shocking. Many young men were discovered to have physical abnormalities that could have been prevented; there was widespread illiteracy; and many maladjusted and psychologically 'sick' men were discovered. It was obvious that the conclusion had to be that American child raising was falling far short of its aims.

During the period of reconstruction after the war, education was once again seen to be the instrument of social progress. 'Prevention' and 'mental health' became magic words and, apart from this, there was also money available, due to the economic revival. Research activities declined again during the economic depression in the thirties. Most of the research was paid for by private funds, one of which was the rich and influential Laura Spelman Rockefeller Memorial (LSRM). One of the most important aims of the LSRM was *parent education* (Frank, 1962; Lomax, 1977; Schlossman, 1981).

In order to achieve this aim, the research centres had to carry out three functions: research, education and distribution of knowledge amongst parents and teachers. The LSRM was extremely active in setting up an organization for combining research with parent education. They subsidized the Child Study Association of America, an organization consisting mainly of women who spread scientific knowledge amongst groups of mothers. The Association of University Women was successfully assisted by the LSRM; child raising as an intellectual and stimulating activity appealed to housewives with a university degree. Congresses were organized, and magazines published, amongst which were *Child Development* and *Child Development Abstracts*; there were also popular pedagogic magazines for parents.

Nursery schools

Within this complex of activities, nursery schools had a place of their own. They were founded within research institutes for research and pedagogic experiments (Davis, 1933; *Preschool and Parental Education*, 1929; Forest, 1929; Weber, 1969: Sears and Dowley, 1963). Children from the age of 18 months spent the greater part of the day, from early morning until well into the afternoon, in these 'human relationship laboratories'. The children could be observed easily in nursery schools, which also presented the opportunity for practical training for future researchers, teachers and advisers on child-care and education. Finally, the parents/mothers could learn, from the nursery school, how to bring up their children in a scientifically responsible fashion. One hundred and fifty years after Oberlin, and 100 years after Froebel, *the scientist had now discovered child centres as a way of raising family upbringing to a higher level.*

The number of nursery schools remained small: in 1930 262 nursery schools were registered, one-third of which were attached to a research or training institute. But their influence was great because of the combination of research, education and parent education. As far as the children were concerned, most attention was paid to medical tests, physical health and social development. 'Habit training' was important: washing hands, hanging up clothes, eating and sleeping together, and so forth. Besides this there was space for outdoor playing, creative activities, reading and so on.

Research in nursery schools

It is impossible to survey the most important research carried out into young children during the twenties and thirties: there was too much and it was too varied. The first book on child psychology appeared in 1931, edited by Murchison. This book contained 275,000 words. Two years later, a new, revised edition was published, owing to 'the great expansion of the field'. This edition contained 405,000 words. These text books gave only a selection of what was happening in the field of child psychology. Apart from American research, these selections include work from Austria (Bühler; Freud), France (Piaget), and Britain (Isaacs). The first thing noticeable to a present-day psychologist is the descriptive character of a great deal of this research. The researchers seemed to want to present a lively image of how children live and develop, with all their individual peculiarities. For instance, Charlotte Bühler (1933), describes how babies react to and imitate one another from the age of 6 weeks; how children from 6 to 10 months old communicate by touching each other, exchanging toys, and pulling and pushing each other. Isaacs (1964), described the emotional relationships of the children in her nursery school: their loves, arguments, friendships, pleasures, jealousies, enmities and sexual curiosity. The subjects discussed by the researchers were more diverse than we are used to nowadays. Under the heading 'emotional development', research can cover humour, children's jokes, boredom, pleasure, curiosity, crying, laughing, sex, jealousy, anger and fear (Arrington, 1943; Jersild, 1947).

However, not all this descriptive research is so lively. A second large research stream was descriptive, but was aimed more at age standards. The best-known researcher in this field was Gesell, but Charlotte Bühler and other less well-known researchers were also active in this area. The aim of this research was to establish the 'normal' development of children in the areas of movement, the use of the senses, memory, language, behaviour with other children and adults, moral judgement, play, and so on. (Gesell, 1940).

To this end, large groups of children were regularly assessed, tested and observed (Lomax, 1977). Development dossiers were kept on nursery-school children. The average scores gave age standards, and a description of the 'normal' stages of development. According to Gesell and others, age standards were important instruments for detecting and preventing abnormalities and illnesses. Therefore, his descriptions were 'behaviour profiles' for the '4-weeks-old', '16-weeks-old', '28-weeks-old', '40-weeks-old', '1-year-old' and so on. (Gesell and Ing, 1943).

Interest in the construction of tests and standardized observation methods (Anderson, 1946) is closely connected to the above. In a bibliography published in 1939, no fewer than 4,000 titles of articles and books about mental testing were mentioned. New instruments were discovered, such as the 'one-way screen' designed by Gesell, which served to observe spontaneous behaviour. Gesell was also one of the first to use film and photographic material. The 'time-sampling' method (observation within a certain time limit) was developed. New statistical techniques were used, such as factor and variant analyses.

A fourth important stream of research was that of the experiment. In nursery schools 'independent variables' were systematically varied, such as the behaviour of the teacher, group variables and the material surroundings. The effects of these on the 'dependent variables', mainly behavioural aspects of the children, were identified and compared with the scores from the control group (Sears and Dowley, 1963; Sjølund, 1973; Swift, 1964). Here are just some of the many possible examples: the effect of dominant and socially integrated behaviour by the teacher; the effect of various disciplinary techniques; children's reactions to experimentally created frustrations; and the effect of attending a nursery school.

Theories on children's development

Theory forming played a very small role in the research carried out during the twenties and thirties. There was little interest in forming concepts, and hypotheses surrounding the mechanisms that form the basis for learning and developmental processes, or surrounding the actual behaviour of children in certain situations. As for theories referred to in research, they were mainly Watson's theories of behaviourism, and Gesell's ripening and growth theory, and to a lesser degree the Gestalt theory, and those of Piaget, Lewin and Freud.

According to John Watson (1878–1957), founder of behaviourism, psychology should be based only on objectively perceptible facts. All behaviour, emotions included, could be conditioned by stimuli from the environment. He was sure he had proved this convincingly by his conditioning experiments, first with animals and later with babies. By subjecting the child and its environment to strict rules, every parent could make his child into what he wanted. Later, Hull, Tolman and Skinner designed variations of this behaviourism, that had a great influence on thought about children's learning and behaviour modification. Just as G. Stanley Hall before him, Gesell resorted to the genetic approach. In his theory the central concepts are 'ripening' and 'growth'. While Watson emphasized the environment, Gesell explained growth with heredity and biological laws. According to him, mental growth is a continuing process of transformation and reconstruction that follows set stages and phases. The environment can block this growth, but can never give it an entirely different course. He said that parents should adapt themselves to the development phase of their child and, if they failed to do this, the child could become ill or abnormal (Gesell and Ing, 1943: 47–58).

The work done by European psychologists was much more theoretical: for instance, Freud's work, which was later expanded in research into the socio-emotional development of young children by Anna Freud and Susan Isaacs, amongst others. In the twenties and thirties, Jean Piaget based his famous theories on cognitive development. In the first American textbook by Murchison, published in 1931, articles by Anna Freud, Susan Isaacs and Jean Piaget were included. However, in the second revised edition, the articles by Freud and Isaacs were scrapped. In the 1946 version, revised by Carmichael, the article by Jean Piaget also disappeared. In the twenties and thirties, Americans wanted little to do with 'speculations', which was how they termed theoretical work. Piaget's and Freud's theories were used only as a reservoir of hypotheses for empirical research. In this way little boys' Oedipal jealousy of their fathers was analysed and statistically processed. Occurrences of Piaget's 'egocentric language use' were counted, and percentages established in nursery schools. But an actual interest in the theories themselves did not develop until the fifties and sixties.

Most of the American research carried out in the twenties and thirties was, in the first place, intended to be useful: how can we improve our education? Improvements of education involved, for Watson, more effective means of controlling children, and for Gesell, controlling them using development standards.

'A healthy detachment'

In the child-study movement under the leadership of G. Stanley Hall, teachers and mothers were consumers as well as producers of scientific knowledge; reading and filling in questionnaires was a popular pastime. During the second child-study movement, relationships were more hierarchical, and scientists were careful to protect their 'science' from lay interference knowledge. Even so, at the beginning of the twenties there was little knowledge to show off. But, just as in Hall's time, this hardly affected faith in the power of scientific knowledge to raise the quality of the American people.

Even though the value of the family was still held in high esteem, particularly by Gesell, there was at the same time doubt about mothers' competence; a scientific upbringing in nursery schools was supposedly better. According to Helen Woolley, director of a large research centre, 'it was just as foolish to rely on maternal instinct when bringing up children as it was to rely on possessive instinct when it came to earning a living for a family' (*Preschool and Parental Education*, 1929: 67). Both of these instincts demand training and education.

Mothers were also felt to be too emotional and irrational: 'By showing too much love, and an unhealthy need of love [in parents], a child who has no concept of independence is produced . . . , and stays clinging to mother's skirt, not only through childhood but for its entire life' (*Preschool and Parental Education*, 1929: 53).

Freud was quoted in order to emphasize the danger of fixation on mother-love. Watson, the behaviourist, was a champion in abhorring mother-love. According to him, 75 per cent of mothers were unfit to bring up children. His book, *The Psychological Care of the Infant and Child* (1928), was dedicated to 'the first mother who brings up a happy child'. According to him, mothers torment their children with their display of love: 'She picks the infant up, kisses and hugs it, rocks it, pets it, and calls it "mother's little lamb", until the child is unhappy and miserable whenever away from actual physical contact with the mother' (Watson, 1928: 17). Watson asked himself whether children would not be happier if they were brought up in institutions rather than at home with their mothers.

Watson represented an extreme point of view amongst psychologists. But the information on upbringing at that time was also based on planning; sleeping and feeding according to time schedules, and particularly not giving in to feelings (Hardyman, 1983: 165–94). One of the most important aims of the nursery school was to encourage 'a healthy detachment' and independence from adults/mothers (Sears and Dowley, 1963: 822–3).

Apart from the distrust felt towards mothers, there were also other arguments for a nursery school, as opposed to a family, upbringing. A few scientists pointed out the bad material circumstances and poverty of parents and children in cities, and for these children the nursery school remained an exception (Davis, 1933: 89–91). There were also arguments reminiscent of our present-day feminism. A female scientist asked herself how ambitious women could be good mothers, if this meant suppressing their talents and work (Forest, 1929: 360–1)? An investigation among nursery school directors showed that relieving parents of their children (child-care) was one of their least important aims (Davis, 1933: 30). Nursery schools were not primarily for working mothers. However, for the mothers with a university background, who were staying at home, active participation in mothers' groups was an alternative career.

In accordance with the high expectations of a scientific upbringing, research work concentrated almost entirely on *the positive effects of nursery schools* at an intellectual level and especially in social/emotional areas (Swift, 1964; Sjølund, 1973). The nursery school was supposed to lead to better social adjustment and greater social ability. This hypothesis was confirmed by various research projects. The children at nursery school seemed to be less reserved and more spontaneous than those staying at home. They were more independent of adults than those at home, but sometimes more dependent on their peers and less obedient. In a couple of research projects no positive effects were observed, but neither were any negative effects apparent.

During the thirties there was an intense debate on the possibility of nursery schools influencing the intellectual functioning of children (Sjølund, 1973: 115–30). Was intelligence hereditary or was it influenced by the environment? In a number of research institutes, the researchers were convinced that their nursery schools raised the children's IQ. Other research institutes challenged this. In 1940 the *Yearbook* of the National Society for the Study of Education was entirely devoted to this 'nature–nurture' debate. During the sixties, a similar discussion once again led to a heated debate about child centres, within the framework of the Head Start project (see Chapter 8).

It is noticeable from our present-day preoccupations that there was no research into the *damaging effects of the nursery school on the mother–child relationship, due to daily separation*. During the thirties, when more attention was paid to children's behavioural and emotional problems in the nursery school, the cause was not to be found in the separation from the mother, but rather in 'mistakes' in the upbringing at home, such as overprotecting, spoiling and neglect (Baruch, 1937; Grant, 1939; Hattwick, 1936). From various research projects it became apparent that nursery schools could have a beneficial effect on children who had previously suffered from psychological problems at home (Bender and Yarnell, 1941; Koshuk, 1947). However, during the forties this philosophy on the value of bringing up young children outside the home was drastically changed: mother-love was rediscovered.

Chapter 6

Regulating emotions
Maternal love, emotional bonds and discipline

There is a very strong case indeed for believing that prolonged separation of a child from its mother (or mother substitute) during the first five years of life stands foremost among the causes of delinquent character development.

(John Bowlby, 1953)

The chief concern of a community should be for its healthy members. . . . The children who are being nurtured in their own homes are the ones that reward; it is the care of these children that pays the dividends.

(D.W. Winnicott, 1950)

MATERNAL LOVE

More than 100 years after Froebel, psychologists discovered maternal love, which was said to have a decisive influence on children's development. The year 1951 can be seen as a milestone in this respect. In that year the English psychiatrist, John Bowlby (1907–) published *Maternal Care and Mental Health*. This report was commissioned by the World Health Organization in order to gain some insight into the plight of orphans and children who had been separated from their parents and been made homeless by events during the Second World War. On the basis of research into children in institutions and hospitals, and research into the pattern of life led by adolescents with criminal records or mental health problems, Bowlby came to the conclusion that a warm, intimate and continuing relationship with a mother figure is an essential precondition for the mental health of children. *Maternal deprivation*, or a disturbed emotional bond between mother and child, was said to cause irreparable damage, not only to the child, but to society as a whole: 'Deprived children, whether in their own homes or out of them, are a source of social infection as real and serious as are carriers of diphtheria and typhoid' (Bowlby, 1952: 157).

In an attempt to curb the 'infection' at source, Bowlby proposed the adoption of a large number of policies: more attention for individual children in institutions and hospitals; the encouragement of fostering; more caution in placing children outside their homes, except in the case of unmarried mothers. According to Bowlby, unmarried mothers were often psychologically disturbed and their children would be better off if adopted by a 'normal family' (Bowlby, 1952: 93–100).

Bowlby advised mothers of young children not to work outside the home. The daily separation could disturb the mother–child relationship, and a disturbed mother–child relationship could later lead to delinquency, anti-social behaviour, neurosis or serious psychiatric problems. Bowlby regarded any form of upbringing for young children outside the home as a danger to public mental health.

Bowlby's report was very controversial in the fifties. It was reprinted in numerous editions, and translated into many languages. The psychologists, once so enthusiastic about nursery schools during the twenties, were, during the fifties, extremely worried about day-care centres and nursery schools for children under the age of 3. What caused this U-turn in thinking about the needs of young children? I will start this chapter with a description of the social backgrounds to the growth of theories in which maternal love plays a central role. I will then go into the contents of the theories; at a theoretical level a connection was made between maternal love, discipline, mental health and the prevention of criminality. Bowlby and other theoreticians worked on a new model for the management of emotions of individuals, in order to achieve a new balance between 'freedom' and 'attachment'.

SOCIAL BACKGROUNDS

There are various hypotheses on the social backgrounds of the 'maternal deprivation' theory and its success. These are connected to the fear of social chaos and dictatorship before and after the Second World War; the problem of dealing with the war victims; the policies with regard to working mothers in a period of rebuilding; and the growth of a new morality of upbringing, the 'fun morality', which gave more space and attention to individual feelings, needs and thought. In the following I will deal briefly with these hypotheses.

The fear of social chaos and dictatorship

Bowlby's report expressed a great anxiety for the social order in the community, which he felt was being threatened by criminality, anti-social behaviour and psychotic and neurotic personalities. With this, Bowlby placed himself in the long line of philanthropists pedagogues and psychologists, who thought that upbringing was both the cause of, and solution to, social instability at times when the phenomenon was highlighted (see previous chapters). Between the two world wars, and in the period afterwards, the fear of social chaos and dictatorship was a recurrent theme in sociological, psychiatric and psychological literature (Riley, 1983; Graebner, 1980; Ehrenreich and English, 1979). The experiences with Hitler's Germany, the Stalinist regime in the Soviet Union and the violence during two world wars had made public opinion sensitive on this theme.

In addition, this was a period in which the churches' decline in power continued, and traditional authorities lost their influence. Studies appeared on the increasing lawlessness of the young. Adorno, who had fled from Nazi Germany, carried out his famous research in the United States into the authoritarian personality (Adorno *et al.*, 1950). Riley (1983) and Graebner (1980) point out that in English and American psychological literature of the time, the child is represented as being unstable and dominated by intense feelings of love and hate; as a potential tyrant or follower of a demagogue. At the same time, the use of external force in upbringing was rejected as being characteristic of the upbringing and educational systems of dictatorships such as Germany or the Soviet Union. The idea of the 'free individual person' had to be defended (Walkerdine, 1984: 181).

Psychoanalysts like Erikson placed emphasis on the importance of a 'basic trust' and 'strength of ego'. According to A.S. Neill, the children in his Summerhill school grew up free of hatred and fear, because they were given absolute freedom to develop all the potential they had 'in' them. Other psychologists held a less optimistic view of human beings. Klein, Winnicott and Bowlby were of the opinion that children know both love and hatred, and that they have to learn to regulate destructive impulses. If they did not, the consequences could be disastrous, according to the *British Medical Journal*, in January 1944:

> in the years from two to five the battle between love and primitive impulse is at its height. . . . Winnicott, Bühler, Isaacs, Bowlby and others all note the turbulent characteristics of the age. . . . Destructive impulses let loose in the war may serve to fan the flame of aggression natural to the nursery age . . . the Age of Resistance may thus be prolonged to adult life in the form of bitterness, irresponsibility, or delinquency.
>
> (Quoted in Riley, 1983: 1)

Psychologists and psychoanalysts all wrestled with the question of how to control the child's aggressive impulses without using authoritarian power and blunt repression. I will return later to the solution suggested by Bowlby and others to this dilemma.

Grief after the First and Second World Wars

According to Newcombe and Lerner (1982), the success of Bowlby's theory must be seen against the background of grief experienced after the First World War. Three-quarters of a million British soldiers had died, leaving behind widows, children, parents and other family. This was at a time when the traditional rituals surrounding grief (black clothing, comfort given by prayer and Church rituals, as well as limited social activity) had been more or less abolished, or had lost a great deal of their meaning due to the Churches' declining influence. Newcombe and Lerner suggest that there was probably a large incidence of emotional disturbance caused by the problems of working through grief and loss. The psychiatrists of the time not only found it difficult to cope with the treatment of the soldiers returning from the trenches, and their relatives, but also with an understanding of their problems at a theoretical level. The older psychiatric theories about the biological causes of mental illness no longer seemed applicable. Neither did Freud's theory of infantile sexual traumas being the cause of all neuroses fit in with the new facts.

More and more psychiatrists sought the cause of emotional disturbances in inter-psychic conflicts (relationships between people), instead of in intra-psychic conflicts. In 1935 Suttie developed a theory that looked very similar to Bowlby's later theories. Suttie emphasized that love and the need for friendship are an autonomous power in development, and just as important as sexuality. Loss and separation could lead to anger, grief and psychosomatic complaints.

It is quite possible that the experiences of the Second World War strengthened the realization of the importance of family bonds, not only because of the new war victims, but also because of the experience of evacuating 700,000 children to the country in Britain alone (Wolf, 1945; Isaacs, 1941). Psychoanalysts like Anna Freud wrote about the problems of 'working through' experienced by children who had grown up in concentration camps, and/or who had lost parents and other relatives (Freud and Dann, 1968).

Motherhood and child-care in the 1950s

A third hypothesis on the background to the success of Bowlby's theory refers to the position of mothers working at home during the 1950s. After the Second World War a period of reconstruction started in Western Europe. In Britain and the Netherlands, 'Restoration of families is restoration of the nation' was a slogan of the time. Feminist studies often point to the similarity of the value orientation in Bowlby's theory, and the ideology of family and motherhood, that was then so apparent. Bowlby's theory was successful because he wrote what a great many people, not only in the field of science, already thought about women (Wilson, 1977; Riley, 1983). However, to assume that women only worked within the family did not correspond with the facts.

At the start of the 1950s, 24.4 per cent of all married women in Britain had a paid job; in the United States the figure was slightly higher, 27 per cent (Myrdal and Klein, 1956: 59). The number of married women with a job grew steadily from the end of the 1920s in Britain as well as in the United States. This process was probably speeded up by the Second World War, when women were recruited *en masse* by the army and war industries, in order to fill the places left open by the general conscription of men (Hesse, 1979). After the war, there was enormous pressure on women to resume their original place in the family. In heavy industry they were more or less totally replaced by men. But, at the same time a new work territory was opened to them, a territory better suited to the traditional 'female' role: in the service industries as typists, saleswomen, administrative workers, social workers and so on. After a short fall-back in 1946, the growth in the number of married women working outside the home continued. To a large extent these were women with older children, but gradually the number of women with younger children taking work outside the home started to grow as well. In a sample studied in 1960, 7.4 per cent of the full-time married women workers had children of pre-school age; of the part-time workers, 14.9 per cent had pre-school children (Klein, 1965: 106).

This growth in the number of women working outside the home remained unnoticed for the most part until the beginning of the 1950s. Social scientists, journalists and possibly a large part of the reading public, laboured happily under the illusion that working mothers had been a temporary phenomena during the war. When the figures became known the main reaction was one of condemnation. The figures were a contradiction of the image of the woman as housewife, or, as Betty Friedan called it 'the feminine mystique' (1963).

During the 1950s there were very few facilities for mothers working outside the home. Measures to make working outside the home unnecessary for women were given priority over measures to enable women to combine working and children: for instance, a family salary for the working man, child allowance and a widow's pension (Lewis, 1980: 165–90).

In Britain during the Second World War, as well as in the United States, all sorts of measures were taken to make the combination of work and children possible; amongst others, crèches and day nurseries were opened. But, immediately after the war in the United States most of the 2,800 war crèches were closed; in England in 1947 the 1,600 day nurseries opened during the war had been halved, and in 1957 only a quarter were left. After the war, mothers had to make their own arrangements for combining a job and children.

The child-care centres which remained had a mainly educational function, but even these were few and far between. Although these centres were praised on all sides, and recognized as an essential part of the educational system, authorities were not prepared to spend money on them. Various economic cuts made in the educational system caused the admission age to be raised and opening hours reduced, making the child-care centres with an educational function unsuitable for working mothers. In 1950 in Britain, only 12.3 per cent of children between the ages of 2 and 5 attended an infant or nursery school subsidized by the government – just as a reminder, in 1900 the proportion was 43.1 per cent (Whitbread, 1972: 112)! In the United States the percentage of children in nursery schools was probably not much higher. In the Netherlands in 1950, 10 per cent of all 3-year-olds and 49 per cent of all 4-year-olds were attending an infant or Froebel school (Singer, 1989: 188).

During the first half of the twentieth century in all three countries, expert counselling and advice for mothers with young children from the lower classes took place mainly through clinics and mothers' classes, which were principally directed towards hygiene, feeding and the prevention of physical illnesses by educating the mothers. Mothers from the middle classes had not only clinics and their own general practitioner, but also mothers' clubs, private nursery schools and, from the 1920s on, child guidance clinics or Medical Child Rearing Bureaux for psychological and pedagogical advice and help with problems concerning upbringing (Levine and Levine, 1970; Ehrenreich and English, 1979).

In all these forms of advice and help, the mother was held to be the chief figure responsible for the physical, and later also the psychological, health of the child. Bowlby's theory supported these attitudes towards motherhood.

Permissive education

Finally, there is a fourth hypothesis on the background to the success of Bowlby's 'maternal deprivation' theory: the rise of the so-called 'consumer society', first in the United States and later in other Western European countries. In advertisements and information about new products, the housewife is, and was, the figure appealed to as the most important consumer: through her pattern of buying and her household work the products are introduced to the other members of the family. Because of the growth in welfare there is also more to consume (Hesse, 1979). The newly discovered needs were not only associated with washing powder, clothing, furniture, household appliances and food. At a psychological and emotional level there was also more space for individual needs, desires and problems. During the 1920s the experiments with education in nursery schools based on psycho-analytical ideas remained limited to a relatively small intellectual and artistic elite. In most of the nursery schools, social adaptation was felt to be more important than the individual emotional development. However, at the end of the 1930s this changed. What had at first been limited to a small elite was now a new American child-rearing morality: the 'fun morality', as Martha Wolfenstein so rightly called it in 1951. Everything had to be fun; what's fun is good; what's fun for the child is fun for the mother.

The fun morality or permissive education, as this was some-times called, freed children and their parents/mothers to a certain extent from the very rigid standards and authoritarian advice on upbringing of the pre-war period (see Chapter 5). Their own, highly personal feelings would be the final criterion.

Take, for instance, the advice given to the parents of crying babies. Froebel thought that parents of a baby who was well looked after should let it cry. Suffering and pain were part of the life created by God; accepting resistance to this would only culti-vate little tyrants (Froebel, 1928). According to advice on child rearing from the 1920s and 1930s in the United States, parents were to check whether their child was crying because of a need essential to health, or because it wanted something. If the latter was the case then on no account was anything to be done; giving in to the child's will would only lead to spoiling (Newson and Newson, 1974).

In informative literature of the 1940s the 'wants and needs are explicitly equalized'. Babies cry because they want attention; they need attention; *they have a right to be satisfied*. A young child cannot be spoilt or receive too much maternal love. Their needs should be followed, and feeding and sleeping schedules should be abolished. From the beginning of the 1940s, similar ideas, coming to the fore in American child-rearing information, gained support from a number of influential books: in the United States, *The Rights of Infants* by Margaret Ribble in 1943; while Bowlby's report in Britain in 1951 has already been mentioned.

Further, one must not underestimate the influence of Spock's *Baby and Child Care*, published in 1946. This book, reprinted and revised many times, translated into very many different lan-guages, is one of the world's best-selling books. Spock used a friendly tone, and was full of understanding for parents/ mothers. Parents/mothers should enjoy their role: mothers and babies 'enjoy' breastfeeding; at bath-time parents are 'delighted' with their baby, and so on. Spock gave very few instructions, considering the period in which he wrote. Mothers had to follow their own feelings. However, as Martha Wolfenstein noted in 1951, this did have a shadow side. Mothers no longer had clear criteria with which to measure whether they were doing right or wrong; everything seemed to depend on nuances of feelings that could not be steered or controlled by wilful decisions. Besides, mothers were expected to invest an enormous amount of emotion and time in their children in order that they might develop 'freely' and 'happily'.

I will return to this last point later. First I will deal with the advocates of this new style of child rearing. How did Bowlby and other supporters of a permissive education view the relation between the child's freedom and the regulation of their behaviour to a socially acceptable form? And how could they combine their preoccupation with the child's aggressive impulses (see page 89), with grief and separation experiences (page 90), maternal love (page 91), and indulgence in upbringing (page 94)?

DUBIOUS LOVE FOR THE CHILD

Feelings of love and hatred for the mother

In the 1950s Bowlby's theoretical thinking was still strongly focused on psychoanalysis, particularly on Melanie Klein's object-relation theory, which was very influential in English psychoanalytical thinking before and after the Second World War. In her theories Melanie Klein (1875–1960) emphasized the first years of a child's life, the pre-Oedipal phase, in which the mother–child dyad plays a central part (Klein, 1975; Segal, 1974). In this she differed from Freud, who emphasized the triadic relationship of father–mother–child. According to Klein, the baby is controlled by innate psychic powers such as love, hatred, envy, guilt feelings, impulses 'to make up again' or 'repair the rela-tionship'. The child feels strongly opposing emotions for the same person: the mother. These conflicting emotions supposedly summon all sorts of counter-reactions, in order to protect the child from disintegration or collapse of the ego.

Children of 2 or 3 months old, who are not yet able to distinguish between themselves and the mother, separate or split 'good' and 'bad' objects from one another. By 'objects', Klein means aspects of a person in which the child invests emotional energy. The good object is internalized (introjection) and forms the basis for a positive 'self'; the bad object is rejected outwards (projection). The child supposedly only wants to absorb good objects, and, as far as it is able, wants to feel 'good' and 'whole'. This is a precarious undertaking full of pitfalls. The child can have the feeling that the projected, bad objects (representative of its own aggression) come back and follow and threaten it. It becomes even more difficult when the child learns to distinguish between itself and the mother as a separate person. The child then has to learn that the good object and the bad object are one and the same person, and then account for the feelings of hatred it feels for someone it loves.

According to Klein, this is what causes guilt feelings and fear for one's own aggression and creates the first forms of a superego. Depression can be a result of denied feelings of aggression; the child can be completely dominated by the fear that the good object in it can be destroyed by the bad object. Luckily, Klein was convinced that beside the feelings of love and hatred, impulses also existed to repair the damage that had (in fantasy) been caused to the loved one. This is the source of human creativity.

Melanie Klein never really studied the possible pedagogic consequences of her theory. Although her work was mainly on the mother–child relationship, she wrote very little about the actual behaviour of mothers. She did not exclude environmental influences on the child, but was of the opinion that even a child growing up in favourable circumstances can develop neurotic disturbances through innate conflicting impulses, and can become entwined in its own fantasies. It is the irony of history which led to psychoanalysts and psychiatrists like Winnicott and Bowlby basing their far-reaching statements on what constituted a 'good' mother, and how 'bad' mothers can ruin their children, on only parts of Klein's theory.

The management of conflicting feelings

In Britain, Bowlby and Winnicott were among the most influential popularizers of the Kleinian philosophy in the field of motherhood and child rearing (Riley, 1983: 80–108). To a large extent they adopted Klein's theories of infantile love, aggression, guilt and anxiety. But, contrary to Klein, Bowlby and Winnicott emphasized the influence of the environment, and particularly the mother, on the results. They designed a management model, in order to control strong emotions. The mother was responsible for the management of the child's psychic energy. According to Bowlby in his 1951 report, she is the *'psychic organizer'* (Bowlby, 1952: 53).

Both Winnicott and Bowlby used many metaphors borrowed from management, animal taming and war. For instance, Winnicott, who had become famous during the Second World War when he gave radio talks, explained to mothers that babies could feel 'furious tigers and lions' inside them, and become afraid of their own feelings. The baby then needs the mother's help in order to learn how to deal with these feelings. It is very healthy for a baby to learn the full extent of his fury. However small and weak a baby is, it does not feel itself to be harmless. It screams, bites, scratches, spits and can even turn blue. 'For a few minutes he really intends to destroy or at least to spoil everyone and everything' (Winnicott, 1981a: 62).

These, however, are only feelings. In his theoretical work, Winnicott explains that the mother should give 'ego support' if the child is in danger of being engulfed by its emotions (Winnicott, 1982). It is impossible for the mother to take all sources of frustration and anger away from her child. A 'good enough' mother is sufficient. She is calm, empathic, tolerant and permanently available, so that the child can always make up to her for all the aggressive fantasies it has had. If the mother is out, the child's fantasies appear to have come true; it has destroyed the mother. This can cause strong guilt feelings and anti-social behaviour. Unconsciously the child provokes punishment by stealing or vandalism, in order to get rid of old guilt feelings (Winnicott, 1982).

According to Bowlby in 1956, the ambivalent feelings towards the mother become unbearable through separation from the mother. The child's intense despair, anger and grief destroy his ability to regulate the feelings of love and hate (Bowlby, 1979b). In his report for the World Health Organization (1951), Bowlby pointed to a study done among children who stole, lied, were aggressive and lacked emotions or feelings of guilt. According to

Bowlby these children had all been separated for long periods of time from their mothers, and had grown up in institutions or with various foster families. In his own research into forty-four young thieves, fourteen of the children appeared to have 'affectionless characters'; nearly all these children had separation experiences. In addition, Bowlby quoted Spitz, who had carried out a great deal of research work in hospitals and institutions, amongst sad, lifeless babies who were very backward in their development. According to Spitz (1945), the damage caused by maternal deprivation is irreparable.

Like Winnicott, Bowlby pleaded for continuous maternal care, and tolerance towards the child's strong ambivalent feelings. This cultivates self-control. Punishment only increases feelings of fear and guilt, which makes the child even more difficult to control. Punishment cultivates rebels. 'As in politics, so with children: in the long run tolerance of opposition pays handsome dividends' (Bowlby, 1979b).

Bowlby viewed maternal love as 'vitamin D' for the child. But there is a catch. Mothers can also be destructive. During the forties, Levy's research into maternal over-protection was published: through unconscious feelings of enmity, mothers suffocated their children with love. Bowlby admitted that mothers occasionally threatened their children with separation – with suicide, running away, taking them to an institution – and that this could also be very bad for a child. According to Bowlby parents often have their own emotional conflicts with which they are unable to cope. Children are the ideal scapegoats on which to project feelings of jealousy, aggression and egoism. Problems like this cannot be solved just by giving more information. Therefore, Bowlby pleaded for expert advice directly after the baby's birth. This was supposed to be a strategic point 'at which to tackle the malign circle of disturbed children growing up to become disturbed parents who in turn handle their children in such a way that the next generation develops the same or similar troubles' (Bowlby, 1979b: 20).

Bowlby, Winnicott, Spock and other supporters of a permissive education were praised for their empathy with the child's soul. But, as far as I can see, they could also be extremely hard, and they had a number of blind spots. They completely overlooked the role of the father. And Bowlby was so preoccupied with separation from the mother that, in 1983, he was forced to confess that he had not noticed child abuse in families. Even so, quite a number of the children he examined in institutions for his report *Maternal Care and Mental Health* (1952) had quite probably been abused within their families (Draijer, 1988).

Winnicott argued that society had to choose to help the relatively healthy children from 'normal' families. The illegitimate children and homeless children were supposedly too badly disturbed to be helped. 'Deprived children', according to Winnicott, were a threat to society, and cost more than they could return. They supposedly lacked any form of self-control and were totally uninhibited. For that reason, he said they would be better off in large institutions, without individual attention and under a dictatorial regime. 'They have to be run by dictatorship methods. . . . Here is *a good form of sublimation for potential dictators*' (Winnicott, 1981b: 139).

Winnicott's plea for large dictatorial institutions for abused children has recently been reprinted in two volumes (Winnicott, 1981b; 1984). Winnicott's and Bowlby's tolerant and empathic approach was restricted to children from complete families with the mother at home. Children who had experiences that totally deviated from the ideal of these two psychoanalysts called forth their fear and aggression.

Immorality and violence

Theories like those of Winnicott and Bowlby were based on an image of the potentially destructive child. In a permissive education with tolerance towards 'natural' impulses, and through maternal love and permanent maternal care, the child would learn to control and regulate its emotions. The lack of emotional bonds, separations and emotionally disturbed mothers would lead to criminality and pathology, and make hard external control a necessity. Through the child, the mother was made responsible for violence and social chaos in the world outside the family, a world from which she was more or less excluded!

This is hermetically sealed reasoning, with enormous power, particularly because it was based on experiences shared by so many people. I am sure that many adults know the fear of losing control of their emotions; because of the two world wars the sensitivity to separations and violence was probably heightened; children can be so badly treated during their childhood that their pain, anger and sorrow are hardly controllable. But what happens when the term 'maternal deprivation' is introduced? All attention is focused on the mother and separations, whilst the violence that more often than not forms the background to institutionalization disappears from sight: wars; discrimination against unmarried mothers who were forced to separate from their children; abuse of children and women within the family. Looked at from this point of view, the term 'paternal violence' would have been more appropriate than 'maternal deprivation'. But in the fifties, family violence had not yet been 'discovered' (by men).

In some ways the new emphasis on maternal love gave women recognition of their value and feelings. This was certainly progress compared with the detached attitude expected from them in the twenties and thirties (Newson and Newson, 1974). Cuddling, playing, following one's own intuition insead of the experts' rules were not only encouraged but were a positive necessity for the children's mental health. At the same time, motherly feelings remained a source of danger. Too much cuddling was perhaps impossible, but there was always the possibility of the wrong sort of love and (subconscious) enmity towards the child. Besides, the child needed the continuous presence of the mother for the first three years. Did the wish to work outside the home mean that (subconsciously) the child was unwanted?

Various American and English authors writing at the end of the fifties and the beginning of the sixties about the mother who works outside the home point out that the recognition of maternal love, and the rise of a 'permissive' upbringing, took place in a period when the level of education received by women and their chances on the labour market were increasing (Myrdal and Klein, 1956; Nye and Hoffman, 1963). The greater tolerance towards children's emotional life went hand in hand with intolerance towards the wishes of mothers, apart from motherhood.

Criticism and discussion

Bowlby's report *Maternal Care and Mental Health* received not only support but also strong criticism. Serious methodological deficiencies were uncovered in the research on which Bowlby had based his work (Van den Berg, 1958; Casler, 1961; O'Connor, 1956; Pinneau, 1955; Yarrow, 1961). The random samples were extremely small; the control groups were not comparable; very little was known about the hereditary burden of the children. Under the heading 'maternal deprivation', experiences of a completely different nature were collected. Having been placed in an institution, the children were not only 'deprived' of their mothers, but also of their fathers, brothers, sisters and their own environment, and they were very often extremely badly cared for. The conclusion that deprivation in early childhood inevitably leads to delinquency and psychopathology was taken to be unproven. The children who were put into institutions because of the war were all younger than 12 years old in 1951. In the retrospective study, the relationship between the separation from the mother and the children's behaviour problems was dubious. On the basis of an extensive study of literature, Clarke and Clarke (1976) declared it to be unproven that early childhood was a sensitive period in which mental health in the further life of a child is decided. According to them experiences at a later age are just as important.

Bruno Bettelheim could not accept Bowlby's view that a bad family was better than a good institution. In 1969 he tried to defend his own institute for autistic children by studying the mental health of kibbutz children, who grew up without close contact with their mothers. In the Netherlands, Van den Berg scorned the idea of compulsory maternal love; that could only lead to artificial and ambivalent behaviour. According to O'Connor (1956) a 'blaming the mother complex' was the basis for Bowlby's report.

There was also much resistance to Bowlby from the behaviourists, who remained dominant in the research world of the United States until 1960. Following in Watson's footsteps, they objected to such an 'unscientific' term as 'maternal love' (Eysenck, 1975). They gave the lack of social and cognitive stimulation as an alternative reason for the children's lack of development. In addition, they continued their experiments with nursery schools, day nurseries and children's homes in order to increase the IQ and learning ability of the children by direct stimulation (see Chapter 5). They remained faithful to their belief in the superiority of expert upbringing and applied science outside the family.

In 1972 Rutter summarized the results of 300 studies on the 'maternal deprivation' theory, and found this theory to be scientifically untenable. However, this in no way meant the end of this way of thinking about the influence of mothers on the emotional and moral development of children. Bowlby rearranged his theories to form the 'attachment theory', which played a large part in the feminist struggle for child-care from the early seventies (see Chapter 8).

Chapter 7

Project Head Start
Efforts to break the cycle of deprivation

> So we figured, we'll get these kids into school ahead of time;
> we'll give them food; we'll give them medical exams; we'll
> give them the shots or the glasses they need; we'll give them
> some acculturation to academic work – we'll give them (this is
> where the name came in) a *head start*.
>
> (Sargent Shriver, 1979)

A HISTORIC CHANCE

In 1968 Bettye Caldwell predicted that the maternal role would be
professionalized before too long. Impressed by the knowledge of
the experts, mothers would admit, 'I am not good enough to do
everything you advise'. Besides, Caldwell was convinced that
more and more working mothers would want a high quality of
upbringing for their children, an upbringing suited to a society
aimed at achievement.

Bettye Caldwell pleaded for child raising as an applied science
in the hands of experts, in the tradition of the nursery schools in
the twenties and thirties. She was convinced that the 'maternal
deprivation' theory was incorrect, and that children at home were
very often deprived. Caldwell and other pedagogic theoreticians
felt that professional upbringing in child-care centres could
increase the IQ and school achievements of children from the
lower social classes.

In the middle of the 1960s, these American psychologists were
given a unique chance to prove their point. The United States
Federal Government made large sums of money available for
interventions in the education of 'culturally deprived' children.
Within the framework of the Head Start project, child-care

centres were established throughout the United States in order to compensate for the shortcomings of upbringing at home. The aim was to offer equal chances to everyone, and to abolish social inequality.

The Head Start philosophy was not confined to the United States, but soon spread to other Western industrialized nations, including Britain and the Netherlands. Project Head Start is one of history's best examples of the cooperation between government and science. It started as a triumph for science, but soon became a hard confrontation between scientists on the one hand and politics and the daily practice of upbringing on the other.

In the first place, scientists were forced to discover that their theories on 'the development' of 'the child' gave them very little to go on when it came to the daily practice of working with different children and parents. This was a threat to their authority as experts on upbringing. Secondly, the ambitious goal of abolishing class and racial differences and inequalities was not achieved. Science was apparently not as powerful as this. In the third place, Head Start stirred up an open political discussion about psychological theories. Was the failure of the project to achieve its high aims caused by the hereditary inferiority of the lower classes and ethnic minorities, or by the power structures at a political, social and economic level, that could not be abolished by upbringing alone? Or were the interventions themselves perhaps too limited; should they be broadened? Head Start forced scientists to reconsider both their theories and the relation between psychology, the practice of upbringing and policies. Some of them, like Urie Bronfenbrenner, pleaded for an ecological approach. By this he meant that in theory as well as in (intervention) practice the relationship network in which the parents and children live should be taken into account, at micro, meso and also macro level. On these grounds he rejected theories about 'the child'.

Others maintained their belief in the superiority of their scientific knowledge, and changed only their strategy. Instead of child-care centres, they chose the mother as the instrument of change. Mothers could protect their children from the consequences of poverty.

In this chapter I will deal with the developmental psychological theories behind Head Start, and their implications on working with children and parents from the lower social classes.

THE WAR AGAINST POVERTY

Unhampered by any historical sense of previous social movements for raising the quality of life for poor children, many Americans – politicians, civil servants, doctors, social workers, teachers, parents and 150,000 volunteers – were carried away by the Head Start project in the mid-sixties. Within five months, six-week summer camps had been organized in more than 3,300 municipalities for 550,000 children under the age of 6. A year later there were 10,000 child centres for 350,000 children. In a short time more than 30,000 teachers were trained. Project Head Start spread across the country like a virus, and inspired people to feverish activity (Zigler and Valentine, 1979: 43–154). The 'vicious circle of poverty' had to be broken.

At the start of the 1960s it became known that there were 9 million families living below the poverty level in the United States. The civil rights movement drew attention to the inequality of housing, work, education and living conditions. Racial unrest and rioting broke out and, according to reports, crime was on the increase. From a report published in 1963 it became apparent that half of all the young men called up for military service had to be rejected, either on the grounds of ill health or because of a lack of education. According to the Kennedy administration, poverty was so widespread that the social stability and economy of the nation was threatened. In 1964 the Federal Government called for a 'war on poverty' in order to improve the economic chances of the poor and minority groups. Initially this policy consisted of creating new jobs, extra education and retraining, and a social security system for the poor at a local level. But then the idea of directing attention to the children arose; at least 50 per cent of the group being targeted consisted of children. Besides, this offered advantages:

> In our society there is a bias against helping adults. The prevalent idea is: 'By God, there's plenty of work to be done, and if people had any get-up-and-go they'd go out and get jobs for themselves.' But there's a contrary bias in favor of helping children.
>
> (Shriver, in Zigler and Valentine, 1979: 52)

The commander of the war on poverty, Sargent Shriver, consulted a number of medical and psychological experts, and the plan was born. The vicious circle of poverty had to be broken by intervening in the upbringing of children at an early age: by taking children out of the (bad) family and placing them in (good) child-care centres. At home the children's development was retarded, which meant that they could not keep up with school work; this increased the chance of unemployment or unskilled labour; poverty increased the chance of complications during birth, as well as the likelihood of growth disorders. Without intervention this circle would remain closed.

The intense interest in children's intellectual development also had a different background. When the Soviet Union launched their first rocket, the Sputnik, in 1958, the United States suddenly awoke to the fact that the Soviet Union was technologically more advanced than they were. The United States became aware of its inadequate scientific elite. This awareness was strengthened by the growing need for more highly trained personnel due to the far-reaching rationalization and automization of the period. 'Hidden talent' from the lower social classes had to be found, while children from the higher classes were to be driven to top achievements by the application of new scientific insights. During the sixties middle-class parents were inundated with success stories about children who could read by the age of 2 and about IQs increasing by 20 per cent a year. 'Children could do better' (Pines, 1967).

INTELLIGENCE: NATURE OR NURTURE?

Project Head Start was based on a combination of political, economic, sociological and psychological theories (Chilman, 1973; Zigler and Anderson, 1979). Among the psychological theories the following basic points were formulated:

1 By nature children can be formed; their growth and development can be strongly influenced by their environment (*environmentalism*).

2 The first years of life are critical. Bad early experiences can lead to increasing problems during later development (*critical period and linear continuity*).

3 Children from lower classes are (culturally) deprived; their parents/mothers are incompetent; by early intervention, possible abnormalities and disorders can be prevented or

cured (*cultural deprivation and preventive intervention*).
4 It is not only social behaviour that is influenced by the environment, but also IQ and cognitive behaviour. Training the cognitive and intellectual capacities increases the chance of success
   at school (*cognitivism*).

These theoretical assumptions were directly contrary to
theories in which poverty and bad school results were explained
by hereditary factors, which had been the dominant theories in
the United States up to this time. The emphasis on hereditary
factors was nourished by the eugenic movement for the improvement of human beings, which also included a number of scientists. For instance, the Englishman Sir Francis Galton wrote in his
Hereditary Character and Talent (1865) that artistic and academic
talents are inherited by the child from its parents. He pleaded for
programmes to make it possible to intervene in the choice of
partners (talented men and women should have children in order
to improve the race), and to intervene in the fertility of poor
specimens, possibly by sterilization.

At the start of the century a connection had developed
between eugenicists and the up-and-coming test psychology.
Under the slogan 'The right man in the right place', tests were
used to measure the 'innate ability' of military recruits and
schoolchildren. In industry there was a great need for tests like
these, caused by the increase in 'middle management', which
meant that the traditional transference of professions from father
to son were no longer adequate; new groups had to be sought in
order to fulfil the demand for skilled workers. But tests were also
used in all sorts of other fields. In some states in the USA, for
instance, children put up for adoption had to undergo a compulsory test to establish whether they were worth adopting.

Until the 1960s in the United States the idea that intellectual
capacities were hereditary remained dominant. For example, in
nursery schools very little had been done to influence cognitive
development. The work done by a small group of scientists in this
field was extremely controversial (Moustakas, 1952; Stoddard
and Wellman, 1940; Swift, 1964). Their success did not come until
years later, during the sixties.

In this connection the study carried out by Skeels in the thirties
is interesting (Skeels and Dye, 1939; 1966). Skeels studied a group
of children brought up in an institution, with an IQ of less than

70. At the age of 2, thirteen of these children were given to mentally retarded women to be looked after; the others remained in the institution as a control group. After a year and a half the IQ of the experimental group had risen by 28 points, while that of the control-group decreased by 26 points. Eleven of the children from the experimental group were eligible for adoption. Thirty years later it turned out that all but two of the experimental group had successfully completed high school, and all were earning their own income. The control-group children were either still in institutions or dead. Think how much money this early intervention has saved the state, wrote Skeels (1966).

During the sixties Skeels's study was often quoted, not only in order to prove the incorrectness of the 'maternal deprivation' theory, but also to underline the importance of compensation programmes.

DEPRIVATION AND RETARDED DEVELOPMENT

Besides experiments with children such as those carried out by Skeels, there were also animal experiments on behavioural learning (Sluckin, 1968). The results of all these experiments only acquired prominence after they had been placed within a theoretical framework by Bloom (1966) and Hunt (1961). Bloom used statistical techniques on psychometric material gathered from longitudinal research started during the twenties and thirties. According to Bloom, it was apparent from these statistics that 50 per cent of the scores of 17-year-olds on IQ tests can be explained by development between conception and the age of 4; approximately 30 per cent by development between 4 and 8 years of age; and 20 per cent between the age of 8 and 17. The first four years of life appeared to be the most influential. For this reason society should prepare its parents better for parenthood. Bad parents cost society a great deal of money.

Hunt (1961) was strongly influenced by Hebb's animal experiments and Piaget's theory on human thought. Hebb had shown that rats kept in laboratory cages in stimulus-free surroundings learned less well than the rats allowed to run around freely. Similar experiments were carried out on dogs and chimpanzees, with similar results. On the basis of these findings Hunt formed the hypothesis that children who grow up 'deprived' also 'learn to learn' less well.

Piaget's theories had been forgotten since the thirties (see Chapter 5). Hunt gave the American public a renewed introduction. In this he emphasized the phased build-up of mental structures, and the child's active role in this. In the sensorimotor period (up to about 1 or 2 years of age), the structure of thought is different from that of the pre-operational phase (2 to 7 or 8 years old). Many 4-year-olds will think that there is more lemonade in a tall glass than in a wide short glass (of equal volume). According to Piaget these children are still led by what they can immediately see. Exterior perception dominates because the child does not yet have the thought structures necessary to correct the appearance.

On the basis of Piaget's and Hebb's research, Hunt postulated three phases which were of *critical importance* for further development. In each phase the child was said to have a different intellectual organization, making different demands on the possibilities for development that the environment should be offering. Up to the age of about 5 months, the baby is said to have mainly homeostatic needs; the environment only needs to offer enough variety to broaden the meaning. In the second phase, the child is said to gain interest in the 'new acquaintance'. In the third phase, from about 12 months, children take an interest in new things and the effects of behaviour. 'Growth motivation' then develops. According to Hunt, it is particularly during this last phase that children from the lower classes are deprived, because of the restrictions placed on children by adults, and through lack of space and opportunities to play. This deprivation was said to lead to a weak cognitive-motivational relationship with the environment: a handicap for life.

HEAD START IN PRACTICE

During the sixties the theories developed by Bloom and Hunt appealed strongly to the American public. But being convinced that IQ can be influenced is quite different from *knowing how to do it.*

In 1964 a 'planning committee' was established for Project Head Start, consisting of thirteen scientists with a medical and psychological background. But, to the anger and despair of the policy makers, these so-called 'experts' were unable to answer the simplest concrete questions, such as the ideal size for groups of children, the teacher/child ratio, and about necessary teaching material and toys (Sugerman, in Zigler and Valentine, 1979: 119). It was not possible to base a teaching plan on Hebb's experiments on rats. Hunt's idea of the 'match' still had to be put into practice. To start with, the 'planning committee' did not wish to go further than a few careful scientific experiments. But the war on poverty programme had hundreds of millions of dollars at its disposal, and this had to be spent in 1964. It was now or never. As with the infant school movement, there were high expectations at the outset, but a lack of expertise when it came to putting the theories into practice.

Within five months a programme had been devised for 550,000 children under the age of 7 in 3,300 municipalities. The Project Head Start that developed from this contained various components and aims:

1 *Health.* Unhealthy children do badly at school. Therefore, all Head Start children were given a medical check-up, including hearing tests, eyesight tests, immunizations and a dental check-up.
2 *Education.* Child centres were to provide low-income children with important learning experiences that they might otherwise have missed, through both centre-based and home-based programmes.
3 *Nutrition.* Hungry children cannot learn. Therefore, every child was to receive daily one warm meal and one snack.
4 *Parent participation.* Parents were to be involved by giving them influence at a local level, and by getting mothers in to help the teachers and social workers on a semi-professional basis. The parents concerned were to learn from Head Start how to teach their own children.
5 *Social and psychological help.* This was help intended for the behaviour problems of individual children, and problems with social security, housing, and so on encountered by individual families.
6 *Employment and career development.* Two-thirds of the staff were to be recruited locally. There were to be special (re)-training schemes for these people with a view to further career possibilities.

The project was to be worked out at a local level, taking into account the specific character of each situation. Alongside this a number of special experiments were set up and guided by universities. Examples of these are the programme devised by Bereiter and Engelmann, in which children were subjected to a strict school training in the use of 'correct' English and the recognition of speech tones and mathematical formulae; Weikart's 'Cognitively-orientated curriculum', which included no specific academic abilities, but where the children had to 'learn to learn"; the Bank Street model, which, like the previous nursery schools, was aimed at the process of developing and learning through playing (Miller, 1979).

However, daily practice in the thousands of local Head Start child centres was a far cry from practice in the university experiments. Often the teachers had undergone only one week of training (Sale, 1979). Some child centres consisted only of one room for playing in; in others the children sat in rows on benches, did school-type exercises, and were taught parrot fashion – the method so criticized by Wilderspin 120 years earlier. Playing with building bricks, painting and playing with water were seen by some teachers more as a reward for good behaviour than an important learning experience. The people who devised the programmes had to rethink some of their ideas.

Jeannette Galambos Stone (1979), author of a guide for working in child centres, admitted how stereotypical her ideas on disadvantaged children had been to start with. Only later did she discover the complexity and resilience of people who live in poverty. Originally, she had not taken into account the fact that these children were not accustomed to classrooms full of toys which they could choose to play with. The approach had to be more structured. Also, the emotional and behavioural problems were greater than those she was used to in middle-class nursery schools.

At a local level attempts were also made to fulfil the other aims of Head Start such as health care, nutrition, parent participation, social and psychological help, and local work. Besides, over the years experiments were centrally initiated to integrate handicapped children, to establish Head Start for elementary school-children ('Follow Through'), parent–child centres for babies and toddlers, and parent education at home ('Home Start'). In practice Head Start was a flexible, comprehensive and multiform programme (Richmond, Stipek and Zigler, 1979).

PSYCHOLOGY AND POLITICS

In 1969 the first evaluation report was published, the so-called *Westinghouse Report*. This was an evaluation of the school achievements of the first generation of Head Start children. The children who had followed only the six-week summer programme scored no higher than other children; children who had followed a one-year programme did somewhat better. Opponents saw this report as proof of the failure of Head Start. The supporters defended Head Start, saying that the evaluation study was unsound, and Head Start's aim was not purely better school results. But the public faith in Head Start was shattered: Head Start had promised a 'revolution'!

After the *Westinghouse Report*, many other evaluation reports followed (Beller, 1985; Belsky and Steinberg, 1978; Bronfenbrenner, 1975; Clarke-Stewart and Fein, 1983; Horowitz and Paden, 1973; Kilmer, 1979; Silverstein, 1981; Smith and James, 1975). From national evaluation reports on the local projects a number of clear and immediate effects became apparent, such as children's school maturity (readiness for school), fewer children with an IQ below 80, a more positive self-image, and more social adaptability (Datta, 1979). Long-term effects, however, were less reliable and too small to enable Head Start to be seen as a powerful means of abolishing social inequalities. The positive influence could still be seen in the first class of the elementary schools, but in the second and third classes this influence had more or less disappeared. Eleven experiments conducted by universities were evaluated in a longitudinal study of the children from the experimental and control groups (Palmer and Anderson, 1979; *As the twig is bent* . . . , 1983). Twenty years after the intervention the researchers established the following positive effects:

1 The programmes raised the scores of IQ tests until up to three or four years after experiencing the programme.
2 In the elementary schools the experimental groups had higher scores in reading and arithmetic tests than the control groups.
3 The children from the experimental groups were less likely to be placed into special education; they also met the demands of the 'high school' slightly more often.
4 Children from the experimental groups had a stronger sense of their own value and higher ambitions; their parents also expected more of them.

5 Indirectly, the experimental programmes raised the children's chance of employment (Lazar, 1983: 461).

So it *was* possible to establish long-term positive effects. But was that enough to maintain political and public enthusiasm for Head Start?

In 1969 Jensen really put the cat among the pigeons with his article 'How much can we boost IQ and scholastic achievement?'. In this article he claimed that IQ and scholastic achievement are 80 per cent determined by heredity; (white) middle-class children supposedly have a genetically determined greater ability for conceptual learning than (black) children from the lower social classes. For the latter group, mechanical learning and drill were supposedly the most effective. According to Jensen, the environmentalism on which Head Start was based was misguided, and this was the reason for the project's failure.

Directly opposing Jensen's racist interpretation were a number of sociological and socio-cultural interpretations under the slogan 'school cannot compensate for society'. Education cannot abolish society's injustice and discrimination. Bowles and Gintis (1976) showed that education actually reproduced class inequality rather than abolished it. Mistakenly, the reason for poor achievement is sought in the individual and his 'shortcomings'. This leads to 'blaming the victim'. The concepts 'deprived child' and 'culture of poverty' are said to be discriminatory because they strengthen the stereotype image of sad little children and (single) mothers who scream, hit and either neglect or overprotect their children (Ginsburg, 1972; Tulkin, 1972).

In 1966 Labov had already shown that poor children do not have a limited use of language, but on the contrary, a different use of language which is just as rich as that of middle-class children (the differentiation hypothesis) (Labov, 1972). The tests for measuring the IQ became the subject of a scientific and political battle. In an historical study, Kamin (1977) showed how IQ tests had been entwined with racist, eugenic and social-political programmes since their development. The favouring of children from the middle class (cultural bias) by the use of IQ tests was thus exposed. Black political groups advised parents and children not to cooperate with IQ and school achievement tests, because the results would be used against them (Gordon, 1979).

Finally, there was a third group of scientists who set them-selves up as *(critical) defenders of Head Start* and other compen-sation programmes. Some of the members of this group had been directly involved with the establishment of the Head Start Project, such as Urie Bronfenbrenner, who was a member of the planning committee of Head Start in 1965; others had been in charge of the various university experiments. In fact, it was their own work that was under discussion. The political result of the debate would be decisive, not only for the continuation of the Head Start subsidies for local projects, but also for their own research finances (Zigler and Valentine, 1979; *As the twig is bent. . .*, 1983).

Their defence consisted of a number of steps. In the first place the pretensions of the project were somewhat lowered: Head Start on its own could not abolish poverty or social inequality. Hereditary factors and unequal social structures played a greater part than was originally thought. But this did not mean that the child's direct environment did not matter; a good environment can be crucial. In the second place they pleaded for an expansion of the interventions. Children need more than education. The defenders of Head Start pointed out that medical care, nutrition and social assistance were all part of Head Start. These com-ponents had barely been included in the evaluation studies. Furthermore, the interventions should take place earlier, from the time of conception, through maternity care and parent/mother education, and not only at the age of 2 or 3; they should also last longer, until after the age of 5 or 6. A total approach was necessary. 'We can safely assume that it is never too early in the child's life to educate families on his needs as he develops . . . the earlier the intervention and the longer it lasts, the better' (Palmer and Anderson, 1979: 460).

Alternatively, why not place the child outside the home com-pletely (Smith and James, 1975)? There were actually three possi-bilities for expansion: expansion of professional upbringing out-side the home; expansion of professional guidance offered to the mother in the home; or a combination of both. At the start of the seventies, for instance, the Milwaukee study experimented with the first possibility. From the age of 3 months every child was given to a trained teacher for whole days; from 18 months they were placed in a small group of two to four children with a teacher. Meanwhile, their mothers were trained to become teacher assistants, and were given courses on household management and child rearing. The results were promising, but the cost per child was too high.

In 1974, Bronfenbrenner launched the concept of 'ecological interventions'. In this the mother at home was given the central role. Bronfenbrenner reasoned that the parents/mothers are present for the entire childhood, whereas the child centres are only available for a few years. However, he did not only call for parent/mother education, but also for ecological interventions in order to enable the mother to be a good mother: better social security payments, employment conditions, medical care, housing, and child centres for older children.

Bronfenbrenner also felt that scientists had looked too long and too hard for 'structures' and 'laws' *within* the individual, without looking at the social reality. Within an 'ecology of human development', more attention should be paid to what people themselves actually want, how they think to achieve their aims and the problems they encounter.

AMBIVALENCE TOWARDS MOTHERS

During the sixties and seventies, Bronfenbrenner's philosophy was not usually applied to intervention projects. In their distrust of parents/mothers from the lower social classes, the twentieth-century psychologists almost outdid their nineteenth-century predecessors. During the preparatory phase of Head Start there was even a short discussion on the desirability of removing children completely from their 'bad environment'. However, the family was felt to be too important for the child (Zigler and Valentine, 1979: 54). Thus, part-time removal from the home, in child centres, and parent/mother education were chosen.

This ambivalence towards parents was also apparent in the thinking about parental participation (Valentine and Stark, 1979). On the one hand, the participation of parents in the Head Start Project was felt to be important for strengthening their involvement. On the other hand, developmental psychologists attached little value to the views of incompetent parents/mothers, who were judged to be in need of guidance from the 'expert staff'. This ambivalent attitude towards parents is also apparent in the sort of research carried out into parent participation. Little research has been done into the power and influence of parents within

Head Start. However, from the little that is known about this, it is apparent that a relatively large number of parents had the authority to make decisions in Head Start committees, and worked as semi-professionals in child centres, in parent/mother guidance, and in social work (O'Keefe, 1979). In places where there was explosive racial tension, parent power was regarded with suspicion, for fear of 'misuse' by militant radical groups. The influence of expert guidance on parents/mothers has been the subject of a relatively large number of studies. Positive effects of this expert guidance on the child's development were sought.

The ambivalence towards parents/mothers also became visible in the evaluations of the centre-based programmes. The evaluation studies looked for positive effects of child centres, which were in fact intended to compensate for the negatively judged home situation. There was little or no study into the possible negative effects of an early separation of mother and child on the development of the child. This is quite remarkable, because at the same time research was being carried out into the detrimental influence of child centres on children of (middle-class) mothers working outside the home (see Chapters 6 and 8), on the basis of the maternal deprivation and attachment theory. In the 587 pages of the book on the history and evaluation of Head Start, edited by Zigler and Valentine (1979), the name 'Bowlby' and the concept of attachment do not appear once. However, from teachers' stories it appears that some children developed a great fear of being separated from their mothers. The separation problem did exist, but was apparently not seen as a contra-indication for the child centre (Stone, 1979).

It was only after the disappointing effects of the child centres became apparent that a start was made in 1972, at a central level in Head Start, to stimulate parent/mother education powerfully (amongst others, Home Start), as a panacea against all social injustice. At a first glance a great faith in parents/mothers would seem to be implicit. Parents have a right to 'awareness of being the most important early teachers of their children' (Honig, 1982).

However, this right carried heavy responsibilities. Some psychologists made mothers entirely responsible for their children's school success (Schlossman, 1978). If the mother was good, the rest did not matter. For instance, Ainsworth and Bell (1974) drew the conclusion from their research that, whereas the environmental conditions associated with socio-economic deprivation have a detrimental effect on cognitive development, a harmonious *infant–mother relationship* can act as a buffer protecting a child from their detrimental effect, and, in fact, *is the single most important factor alleviating socio-economic disadvantage.*

(Italics added)

Within this vision, the mother is valued as a buffer against the detrimental influence of poverty on her child. But, at the same time, it is said that these mothers in particular are the ones who fall short on this point. Therefore, parent education and expert guidance are necessary. Without such help, these mothers would be unable to act as buffers.

Not all advocates of parent/mother education were insensitive to the living conditions and objective possibilities available to mothers. Chilman (1973) and Bronfenbrenner (1975) emphasized that parent/mother education should be coupled to financial assistance and other 'ecological interventions'. The victim (the mother) should not be blamed for everything. From this vantage point a number of experiments were set up (Ramey, Dorval and Baker-Ward, 1983).

The parent/mother education programmes within Head Start differed in their range. The programmes devised by Ira Gordon and Phyllis Levenstein during the sixties and seventies were more or less exclusively aimed at changing the mother. In Gordon's programme, mothers with children up to 3 years of age received weekly home visits from specially trained women from the same social class as the mother (Jester and Guinagh, 1983). The aim was to teach the mother how to play with her child. The games were based on Piaget's theory of the sensori-motor period of development. In Levenstein's programme, the children were older (between 20 and 43 months). Their mothers received weekly home visits from the 'toy demonstrator', who, using a particular toy or book, would explain how these could be used to stimulate the child's language and cognitive development. The mother was allowed to keep the toys and books in order to practise. To start with, the toy demonstrators were qualified social workers, but these were later replaced by (middle-class) volunteers and specially trained semi-professional women from the same social background as the mother. Women from the same group appeared to have the advantage of making the mothers feel more at home with them. However, a disadvantage was that very often their play instruction was too rigid, and that they had little patience with the mothers and were more inclined to play with the children themselves (Honig, 1982).

The Home Start demonstration projects were more broadly set up. Here too there were weekly home visits by semi-professional women from the same background. The 'home visitors' offered help in the fields of nutrition (cooking, writing shopping lists), health (accompanying the mothers to the doctor, dentist, hygiene), social assistance (organizing transport, financial assistance), and child rearing. The latter included going to the library, reading to the child in the mother's presence, and teaching the mother how to make everyday experiences into important learning moments for their children. However, the staff in charge very soon discovered that if they wanted to reach the mother, they could not ignore the rest of the family.

Each week brought Home Visitors into rooms where children and parents played and lived; into kitchens where there often wasn't any food for the evening meal; and into complicated affairs where husbands or wives were ill, in-laws needed help or older children were plagued by emotional or physical problems.

(O'Keefe, 1979)

In the mid-seventies, 'home training' the mother seemed to be the answer to everything within Head Start. But at the start of the eighties this popularity was waning. From a longitudinal study carried out on the eleven university experiments, it appeared that home training was no more effective than centre-based interventions (*As the twig is bent* . . . ,1983). Sometimes it was hardly possible to note any positive effect of home training on the children (Madden, O'Hare and Levenstein, 1984; Scarr and McCartney, 1988). The research results, however, are far from unanimous.

The problem is that we do not know why a programme sometimes works and sometimes does not. Does it work because of the teaching plan, the personality of the teacher or 'home visitor', the extra attention, or through the idea that something good is happening to the child? These questions raise more fundamental questions on the (so-called) superiority of the expert's knowledge, and the almost total lack of theory forming and research into how parents learn and live with their children (Gray and Wandersman, 1980; Clarke-Stewart and Fein, 1983).

THE MOTHER AS TEACHER

Why did the advocates of home training for mothers think that it would be advantageous for the cognitive development of children? According to Bronfenbrenner (1975) this was because

> the mothers are recognized in their role as the first teacher of their child, and they learn techniques to enable them to influence their child's behaviour; this strengthens the feeling of responsibility and the mothers' positive self image.
>
> In the programs, interactions between mother and child are encouraged. The child experiences that it can influence its mother and environment. Not only is the cognitive development encouraged by this, but also the child's attachment to the mother. The latter strengthens the child's motivation to learn from the mother.

In many studies a correlation was found between the IQ scores of a child and aspects of maternal behaviour (Clarke-Stewart, 1977: 25). On the basis of this an image developed of 'optimal care'. Optimal maternal care would be apparent in the following: looking at the child, laughing with it, talking with it, playing together and offering toys – and all this at exactly the right moment, without restrictions, and through reacting sensitively and responsively to the child. Attachment theory had a great influence on this image of 'optimal care' within mother/parent programmes (see Chapter 8).

In a playful way, mothers could teach their children all sorts of things. For instance, shopping in the supermarket opens up all sorts of teaching possibilities for practising concepts such as 'big' and 'small', 'square' and 'round', and colours. During everyday chats about pets or toys, the children's language can be expanded by asking questions and answering the why's, what's and wherefore's (Schachter, 1979; Tizard and Hughes, 1984). The household offers numerous opportunities for teaching and learning. But mothers must make use of all these opportunities.

Mothers from lower social classes apparently failed to do this. Instead of creating an environment in which children could discover things for themselves, they gave more instructions. They were more rejecting, and responded more often with 'no', 'don't do that' and 'that's not allowed', without explaining why, and without attempting to interest the child in something else. When dealing with small problems, they were more inclined to give ready-made answers without helping the child to look for alternatives (Clarke-Stewart, 1977; Bee, Egeren, Streissguth, Nyman and Leckie, 1969; Schachter, 1979).

According to Schachter (1979), mothers with a higher level of education spontaneously follow the theories of Dewey and Piaget. They behave like teachers in a child-centred nursery school. This seems to hit the nail on the head. The mothers with a higher level of education, studied by Schachter, had made their home into a learning environment, a sort of nursery school in which the design and the activities are intended to give children the opportunity to experiment and discover.

In previous chapters, I have shown how it took 150 years for the 'socially empty space' which the first infant school originally was, to become filled with material, games, playing and building corners, and so on. I also showed that middle-class women/ mothers were often the propagators of this new 'child-centred' way of working in the kindergartens and nursery schools, and in the family upbringing at home. The new pedagogic approach made household work and the children intellectually more interesting. These women had enough time and money to turn low-valued household jobs such as washing-up, cooking and cleaning into highly valued pedagogic activities.

During the seventies a new step was made in the development of a child-centred upbringing. It was not only the child centres that had to be totally child-orientated, and a children's room and children's games were no longer enough: *housekeeping itself must be made into a pedagogic game.* Mother had to turn her work into a children's game, offering learning possibilities for encouraging the child's development (Walkerdine and Lucey, 1989). This was, and is, probably partly due to the mother's directly experienced need not to have to say 'no' all the time, that she and the children must not constantly get in each other's way, and that – at the same time – she must teach the children as much as possible. But housekeeping is not only a game, it is also work that has to be done. Mother is not only a nanny.

In 1974, Bronfenbrenner had already come to the conclusion that the home visitors programme was particularly attractive to the upper level of the lower social class. If mothers were already overworked, there was no room left for the programmes. Researchers often had great difficulty in finding mothers for their programmes, and half the mothers stopped the programme prematurely (Madden, O'Hare and Levenstein, 1984; Ramey, Bryant and Suarez, 1985).

Differences in standards and values also formed an obstacle for the home training (Gray and Wandersman, 1980). The middle-class home visitors found attitudes towards boys and girls too stereotyped, and the mothers too authoritarian. For instance, Schachter (1979) tried to reduce the number of 'no's' uttered by the mothers by teaching them new techniques: putting something out of the child's reach, explaining, or offering the child an alternative. Mothers were taught to exercise as little visible power as possible over their children. This caused intense emotions and strong resistance from some mothers. They did not want to spoil their children, and held to their authority: 'When I say no I mean no'.

These women, who refused to give up their direct visible power over their children, touched the core of a problem associated with the standard model of 'good mothering': that the mother has to put herself totally at the service of her child, and relinquish any visible or perceptible wishes or work of her own. The resistance by mothers from the lower social classes does not necessarily point to ignorance or powerlessness through over-burdening (Walkerdine and Lucey, 1989). It can also mean that they are protecting their own feeling of value, derived from their household work, and their directly visible authority over their children.

Chapter 8

Attachment theory and day-care

Sensitive mothers and the feminist struggle for child-care facilities

The sensitive mother is able to see things from her baby's point of view. She is tuned-in to receive the baby's signals: she interprets them correctly, and she responds to them promptly and appropriately.

(Ainsworth, Bell and Stayton, 1971)

The mother who usually bears the brunt of parenting during the early months or years, needs all the help she can get – not in looking after her baby, which is her job – but in all the household chores.

(Bowlby, 1988)

THE RISE OF ATTACHMENT THEORY IN THE SEVENTIES

During the sixties, child-care facilities within the Head Start Project were strongly advocated by psychologists. However, psychologists in the field of emotional development maintained their negative judgement. Whilst the positive effects of child-care centres on the cognitive development of 'disadvantaged children' were sought within the Head Start Project, the negative effects on the emotional development of the child were being examined in the case of the children of (middle-class) women working outside the home. The latter research was mainly based on the 'attachment theory' developed by Bowlby in cooperation with the American psychologist and researcher Mary Ainsworth, after the failure of the maternal deprivation theory.

In this chapter I will first describe attachment theory and the attachment research carried out on child-care centres. Then I will show how a design for the 'management of emotions' is offered within attachment theory; a design in which the separation of tasks between the caring parent/mother and the working parent/father plays an important part.

A STRONG ATTACHMENT TO THE MOTHER: THE SECURE BASE

In his attachment theory, Bowlby distances himself from the psychoanalytical concepts on which the maternal deprivation theory was based. The ambivalent emotions of love and hate felt by the child towards the mother are no longer of importance. The child's fantasies about the mother and defence mechanisms disappear from the centre of his theoretical philosophy. The reason for mental disturbances is no longer the mother (figure) who has been inadequate in helping her child to regulate emotional conflicts, but is now the mother (figure) to whom the child is insecurely attached. In his attachment theory, Bowlby states that every newborn baby arrives in the world with an *innate tendency to remain close to his primary care-taker*, and that adults – mothers in particular – have an innate tendency to remain close to the child and protect it (Bowlby, 1988: 120–3).

Bowlby hypothesized that this tendency to remain close developed during evolution: the children's chances of survival were heightened. A newborn baby can do little other than cry when seeking close contact. Later, in relation to the mother, the child learns more active methods of gaining her attention: laughing, babbling, sitting, grabbing, throwing, crawling, walking and so on. The child forms a 'working model' or cognitive scheme of the environment (mother, other attachment figures, strangers), and its own behavioural alternatives for achieving its goal: close contact with the mother figure when it is feeling tired, afraid, sad or unsafe.

Besides the need for close contact, the attachment theory also supposes a second innate tendency: *the urge to explore the outside world*. This supposedly developed during the evolution of man, and also had a survival value: contact with the outside world is necessary for making a living. Bowlby hypothesized that the infant's urge to explore and play, which takes him away from his mother, counteracts his need for safety through proximity. The mechanism providing a balance between infants' need for safety and their need for varied experiences was called by Bowlby 'attachment'.

Attachment is a highly evolved system of regulation geared to produce a dynamic equilibrium between the mother–child pair. At first the mother bears the greatest responsibility for maintaining the equilibrium of the attachment system. If the mother is 'sensitive', 'responsive', 'available' and responds promptly and adequately to the child's signals, a secure attachment will develop (Ainsworth, Bell and Stayton, 1971; Bowlby, 1988: 119–36). The mother of a securely attached baby provides a secure base from which the baby can make exploratory excursions, coming back every so often to renew contact before returning to exploration. At times of distress the baby trusts that proximity with the mother can be sought and found. A sensitive mother gives the child the *feeling of having control over her behaviour*; the child builds up the expectation that the mother's behaviour is predictable and can be influenced. This lays the basis for a feeling of self-confidence (Ainsworth and Bell, 1974).

Children of non-sensitive and unavailable mothers will cling to them from fear, or pretend they do not need her. They do not develop self-confidence or a feeling of having a secure base. There are two types of insecurely or anxiously attached children. *'Anxious/avoidant'* children are the ones who cling to their mothers and are unable to use her as a base for exploration. They respond with fear to strangers, and with intense grief if the mother or attachment figure goes away. The other type is the *'anxious/resistant'*, who refuse the protection and close contact with the mother or attachment figure, and are defensively independent. Their apparent indifference and quasi-exploration mask in reality a strongly activated attachment behaviour system. But they do not seek close contact because, in the past, they have been deeply disappointed.

According to Bowlby, all separations from the mother or attachment figure before the age of 3 are a potential risk to the child. An absent mother is not sensitive and available, and the child experiences the feeling of having no control over her proximity. The child becomes anxious or angry and develops an insecure attachment. After the age of 3, the actual presence of the attachment figure is no longer continually necessary. The child has by then internalized the mother image and absorbed it into the 'working model'. It can trust the mother figure to return if it needs consolation or protection. According to Bowlby, all the child's later relationships will be modelled on this first attachment relationship with the mother figure. This theory forms the core of the so-called 'monotropy hypothesis'.

A STRANGE AND HOSTILE WORLD OUTSIDE THE HOME

According to the 'maternal deprivation' theory, the mother must help the child to regulate contradictory emotions of love and hate. Bowlby introduced a new contradiction in the attachment theory, that between close contact and exploring the outside world, which also had to be regulated with the help of a mother figure. Bowlby compared the exploring child to an army at war. Without a home front, waiting and offering comfort after defeats, the commanding officer on foreign territory would never dare to take any risks (Bowlby, 1988: 11).

According to Bowlby the mentally healthy mother is protected by the father from the outside world, to enable her to create the secure base for her child (Bowlby, 1979a, 105; 1988: 1–19). Bowlby assumes that the separation of work/exploring the outside world, and close contact/safety within the family, are genetically anchored, universal human facts. But what happens if the home front, in this case the mother, herself undertakes all sorts of things outside the home? On the basis of the attachment theory, Bowlby once again pronounces his fears about the effects of mothers working outside the home on children under the age of 3.

Is a day-care centre or the child-minder's home really a strange and hostile world for the child? And are infants really put at risk by daily separation from their working mothers? Researchers have tried to answer these questions by comparing the mother–child relationship of children at home to that of the children of working mothers. The quality of the relationship was mainly based on a single assessment procedure: the *Strange Situation Test*, designed by Mary Ainsworth (Ainsworth and Bell, 1974).

In the Strange Situation Test, mother and child are placed in a room full of toys suitable for a 2-year-old. Then situations are created which are (slightly) threatening to the child: a strange man/woman comes in; mother leaves the room, leaving the child alone with the stranger; mother comes back and the stranger leaves; mother leaves again and the child is alone; the stranger comes back; mother comes back. The child's behaviour in these different situations is scored according to exploratory behaviour, reactions to mother's departure and to the stranger, and reactions to the mother's return. These scores result in a classification of the child as either securely or anxiously attached, with further sub-divisions in a number of sub-categories. Initially, more attention was paid to emotions (anger, ignoring, crying, looking for consolation); in current research, the emphasis is laid on the organization of the search for close contact and exploration (the working model). Neither the mothers' reactions to these strange situations nor their influence on the children were noted.

During the seventies mainly simple research models were used consisting of a small group of between ten and thirty children in care outside the home between the ages of 1 and 3, and a control group of children who stayed at home. The scores on the Strange Situation Test were compared and sometimes supple-mented with a few other tests, questionnaires and observations in the home and the child-care situation (Belsky and Steinberg, 1978; Hock 1978, 1980; Hoffman 1974, 1979).

In various reviews published round about 1980, the conclusion was reached that child-care outside the home need not have a damaging effect on children (Belsky and Steinberg, 1978; Kilmer, 1979; Rutter, 1981; Silverstein, 1981). Children in day-care were just as securely attached as children who stayed at home. Mothers working outside the home who find satisfaction in their work, have a good day-care system, are not overworked and do not feel guilty are just as good for their children as the stay-at-home mothers, and sometimes better (Hoffman, 1974, 1979). Children appeared well able to develop an attachment with the care-taker or teacher, but most of them preferred their mother at times of stress (Farron and Ramey, 1977; Cummings, 1980; Ricciuti, 1974). From this research it became apparent that daily recurring separations did not stand in the way of attachment to the mother. However, the reviews of the research in the seventies were also strongly critical of the validity of the evidence of the impact of day-care on children. Most of the evidence derived from studies of only high-quality, university-based day-care, which is not representative of the alternative care arrangements utilized by most parents.

Besides, the measurement of the effects on children had been restricted to the Strange Situation Test carried out in laboratory conditions. Or, as Bronfenbrenner (1979: 19) put it: 'much of developmental psychology, as it now exists, is the science of the strange behavior of children in strange situations with strange adults for the briefest possible periods of time.'

There was a growing fear that there were probably more subtle differences between stay-at-home children and children in care outside the home, and that these had remained invisible in this research. Extra caution was necessary.

CONSTANT WORRY ABOUT POSSIBLE NEGATIVE EFFECTS OF DAY-CARE VERSUS CONTINUED CONCERN FOR GOOD PROVISIONS

From the end of the seventies a number of situational factors were taken into account that could influence the development of children of working mothers. Clarke-Stewart and Fein (1983) noted factors that could influence the quality of child-care facilities: the size of the group; gender, age, training, experience and attitudes of the staff; the place where the child-care is situated (at home, with a child-minder or a university-based child-care centre); children's special characteristics (such as age, temperament, life history, level of development and special needs).

Important characteristics of parents are: behaviour, attitudes and social-economic status. Powell (1980) added variables concerning the relationship between parents and teachers or parents and caretaker. Grotberg (1980) mentioned government policy; and according to Goossens (1986) and Hochschild (1989) the roles taken by the mother and father in the household chores also have a great influence.

Through more complex research designs an enormous amount of empirical data has become available, which can now be better processed using computers and advanced statistical techniques. However, the drawback to this is the fact that the great number of variables are difficult to interpret with the help of current theories. For instance, attachment theory is based on an evolutionary perspective, and not on analyses of the socio-cultural context. Therefore, this theory cannot offer a conceptional framework for socio-cultural factors. A discrepancy has arisen between the results of different research work. For instance, Benn (1986) found that mothers who returned to work significantly early during the first year after birth often had more securely attached sons than women who returned to work later.

Vaughn, Govers and Egeland (1980), however, found quite the opposite.

When interpreting research data, the attitude of the researcher with regard to maternal employment seems to be decisive. In the present discussions two political positions can be distinguished. One group considers infant day-care to be a risk factor (Belsky and Rovine, 1988; Vaughn, Govers and Egeland, 1980); the second group wants to see an end to all prejudice against the working mother and day-care (Phillips, 1987; Clarke-Stewart, 1988). The latter researchers point out that the percentage of working mothers with children under 4 years of age is rising in the United States from 20 per cent in 1965 and 29 per cent in 1975 to 48 per cent in 1982 (Clarke-Stewart and Fein, 1983: 933). In this situation the only relevant question is: *how can we organize child-care outside the home so that it is good for both parents and children?*

Following a study carried out by Belsky and Rovine (1988), a conflict arose between these two viewpoints. What happened? In their research, Belsky and Rovine had found that children who were separated from their mothers for more than twenty hours a week before their first birthday were more often anxiously attached to their mothers and showed more avoidance behaviour when their mothers returned after the separation in the Strange Situation Test. Besides, the sons of mothers working full-time (more than thirty-five hours) ran a higher risk of also having an anxious attachment to their fathers. The mothers of these little boys had a greater career orientation and a more limited inter-personal sensitivity. The researchers also quoted other research with similar results (Vaughn, Govers and Egeland, 1980; Schwartz, 1983; Barglow, Vaugh and Molitor, 1987; Jacobsen and Wille, 1984). Belsky and Rovine concluded that child-care outside the home for more than twenty hours a week formed a risk factor.

Others find this conclusion far too simple (Clarke-Stewart, 1988; Fein and Fox, 1988; Phillips, 1987; Richters and Zahn-Waxler, 1988; Singer,1989; Thompson, 1988). In the first place, the researchers' concern is strikingly one-sided. For instance, the daughters of full-time stay-at-home mothers (housewives), were apparently more often insecurely attached to their fathers. Belsky and Rovine ignored this result because it was supposedly 'inexplicable'. But can the anxious attachment of the little boys to their fathers be explained by mothers working outside the home? Other criticisms of the research are that only the personality traits of the mother were looked at, and not those of the father; and no attention was paid to the quality of the care. Besides, statistical connections are not the same as causal ones; there is no knowledge as to whether the one factor (full-time working mother) causes the other (anxious attachment to father).

But whichever way it is, more children were scored as 'anxiously attached to their mother' in the group of children in care outside the home for more than thirty-five hours a week (47 per cent of the 'full-time non-maternal care', compared with 25 per cent of the 'full-time maternal care'). An important question is: how serious is this for the children involved? Does 'avoidance behaviour' point to 'anxious attachment'? Or is it quite possible that the children of working mothers are used to separations from the mother, do not find the situation 'strange', and therefore do not seek approach? It is probable that these children would show secure attachment behaviour in situations which they experience as 'really' unsafe.

Another possibility is that the children in care outside the home develop a different 'working model'; in other words, they develop a different way of feeling safe, one which is better suited to their own situation. The *meaning of a healthy secure attachment* can be different for children growing up in different situations. From research into attachment carried out in West Germany, the Netherlands, Sweden and Japan, it became apparent that in these countries the division between securely and anxiously attached children is different from that among American children; when more studies were carried out in one country there were also large differences (Van IJzendoorn and Tavecchio, 1987: 18; Van IJzendoorn and Kroonenberg, 1988). Inter- and intra-cultural differences can exist, which are, in themselves, just as 'healthy' (Clarke-Stewart, 1988; Thompson, 1988).

Critics who reason from a positive attitude towards child-care outside the home reject simplistic conclusions such as those of Belsky and Rovine. The whole question of whether child-care outside the home for more than twenty hours a week is bad for children is misguided. The question should be: under what circumstances can certain results be associated with certain patterns of 'non-maternal' care, and to what extent and why? At the present time we have no answer. The phenomenon is too complex and, as yet, there is very little theorizing on this subject (Phillips, 1987; Richters and Zahn-Waxler, 1988).

THE LIMITATIONS OF ATTACHMENT THEORY

Not all attachment theoreticians have a negative attitude towards child-care outside the home. In the Netherlands, Van IJzendoorn, Tavecchio, Goossens and Vergeer (1982) have introduced the so-called 'extension hypothesis'. According to them, Bowlby's idea that a child attaches itself especially to one mother-figure, the so-called 'monotropy hypothesis', is not confirmed. Research shows that children can be equally attached to both their fathers and their mothers. Van IJzendoorn and colleagues actually advocate more attachment figures, because the psychopathology caused by an anxious attachment to the mother can be compensated by secure attachment to the father or other care-giver.

For mothers working outside the home, the extension hypothesis is probably a welcome amendment to Bowlby's theory. However, another question is: what insights does this amended attachment theory offer into the relationships between parents, children and substitute care takers at a social and emotional level?

According to the extension hypothesis, children can be equally attached to both their parents and their care-taker or teacher. However, I am convinced that there must be a psychologically relevant difference between the way a child will attach itself to its parents and the way it becomes attached to its teacher or care-taker. After all, the latter will only be part of the child's life for a few years.

In attachment theory, a dyadic model of one child and one care taker is used. In the case of multiple attachments, more dyads are studied as if they were unconnected. Therefore, the theory cannot offer an insight into the dynamics of the relationships between parent(s), child(ren) and care-taker(s). Attachment theory is mainly concerned with the child's well-being, and hardly at all with that of the mothers, fathers or care-takers. Instead of a dyadic model it would be better to use a triadic model or 'n-person' models. I will give two examples.

First, a 2-year-old has a good relationship with his mother. Then a baby brother is born. In the year that follows, the child experiences all the emotions of love, rivalry, disappointment, anger, curiosity and pride in his own 'being big' in relation to his mother, father and baby brother. A process like this cannot possibly be described as the result of the sensitivity, responsiveness and availability of the mother and possibly the father. It is a complex group process, in which all four participants play an active role (Dunn and Kendrick, 1982).

Secondly, two teachers together take care of eight children. Is the emotional security of the children in this case dependent on the responsiveness and sensitivity of the two teachers to each of the eight individual children (eight dyads multiplied by two)? It is more probable that the care-taker's ability to organize a group by introducing rules and habits, and by organizing the available space, is just as important for the emotional climate of the group. Another important factor is the way in which care-givers stimulate relationships between the children and make use of the latters' inclination to imitate one another. Van der Laan and Tubbergen (1986) found, for instance, that children in a baby group become attached to one another, and find support from one another when they move from the baby group to the toddler group. It does not seem to bother them that they have to get used to new care-givers.

As early as the twenties, Susan Isaacs pointed out the importance of contemporaries for young children. The feeling of 'being together' with contemporaries can apparently give even very young children a feeling of safety (Isaacs, 1933: 217–18). Insight into relationship networks between parents, children, caretaker/teacher is necessary in order to understand the emotional development of mothers/parents and children who, from the age of 2 months, grow up in two completely different situations.

The same applies to possible (sub-)cultural differences in children's attachment development. Perhaps children who stay at home develop differently from children receiving care outside the home. These phenomena are difficult to conceptualize within a theory based on universal development grounded on evolutionary factors.

EMOTIONAL DEVELOPMENT IN A SOCIAL CONTEXT

During recent years a number of American researchers have taken the difference between the home situation and the care situation as the starting point for their research (Hess, Price, Dickson and Conroy, 1981; Katz, 1980; Powell, 1980b, 1984). From this basis they have endeavoured to explain the differences in relationships and styles of upbringing. They pointed out that teachers had undergone expert training, and mothers had not. During training, child-orientated work is learnt, creating situations for learning by playing, avoiding punishment, stimulating independence, and so on. The teachers' main task is the care of the children, whilst the mother also has to look after the housekeeping and her husband in a house that has to be comfortable for adults as well as children. Teachers work with colleagues, within an institution that restricts them through rules and regulations about working hours, sleeping and feeding times. Contrary to this, the mothers work on their own, and have more space to make up their own timetable.

The character of the emotional relationship with the children is also quite different. Mothers and fathers have a bond for life with their children, whereas the bond between teachers and children is only temporary. Teachers develop a similar bond with a new group of children every time the group changes. Therefore, teachers are likely to maintain more distance.

From the above differences, Hess, Price, Dickson and Conroy (1981) explained the differences they encountered in their study between the behaviour of teachers and parents' behaviour towards children. Teachers appeared to be less restrictive and had more contact with the children in play situations. Mothers had more caring contacts and made higher demands on their children with regard to socialization. According to the researchers, because of the restrictions of their situation and their other responsibilities, mothers had less patience and demanded more obedience more often. They could not, as the teacher was able to, refer to the impersonal group rules and agreements made with the children. From the same situational differences it is understandable that other studies, like the one undertaken by Tizard and Hughes (1984), found that 4-year-olds at home with their mothers played more freely, and talked about a broader number of subjects than with their teachers at school. The children had more shared experiences in a family context which they could talk about with their mothers. Rubenstein, Pedersen and Yarrow (1977), found a similar difference: babies' mothers were more encouraging and responsive than the care-taker who came to the house. Mothers had a more personal relationship.

When looking at the differences between child-care at home and child-care outside the home, the question soon arises as to what is better for the child. But prior to this is the question: is it necessary for mothers and teachers to develop the same social-emotional relationship with the children? Lilian Katz (1980) thinks not. According to Katz, parents have an involvement with their children which is difficult to replace. They are prejudiced and sometimes irrational. Because of this children know that they matter, and that someone will continue to unreasonable lengths with them. On the other hand, teachers offer a more rational, stable and predictable social system, in which children are able to find more emotional peace in which to play with one another.

Katz is of the opinion that in child-care outside the home, the basis should be the differences between parents and teachers. Role confusion, according to her,causes a great deal of suffering. Parents are too often given advice by teachers which presupposes a greater rationality and planning ability than they actually have, resulting in guilt feelings and uncertainty. Teachers who want to be 'mother' and over-invest are soon burnt out. From this point of view, interest has grown among researchers during recent years for the 'triangular relationship' between parents, children, teacher (Bradbord and Endsley, 1980; Powell, 1977, 1978, 1980b; Fein, 1980; Ramey, Dorval and Baker-Ward, 1983; Turner and Zigler, 1987). On the one hand parents and teachers share the intimate care of a young child, and they have to come to agreements about sleeping times, eating habits, toilet training and other things that were previously part of the family's private life. On the other hand, parents and teachers have a different sort of relationship with the child.

According to the psychoanalyst Sally Provence (1982), contact with the parents places high demands on the teachers. They have to learn how to handle their own feelings of jealousy, as well as anger if they feel the parents are failing the child in some way. The quality of the parent–teacher relationship is, to a large extent, critical for the emotional climate in which the child grows up.

What is the effect on children of growing up from the age of 2 months in two or more different social-emotional systems? Very little research has been done into child-care outside the home from this point of view. One example of this sort of research is that carried out by Rubenstein and Howes (1983), in which comparisons were made over a number of years between stay-at-home children and children in child-care outside the home. From their study it became clear that the children who were in child-care outside the home from the age of 18 months had more positive interactions with adults than when they were at home. There was more laughter, less crying and fewer reprimands. The researchers point out, as did Hess, Price, Dickson and Conroy (1981), that the two teachers only have to look after the children and encourage the children to play and imitate. Perhaps this social situation is more fun than the isolated situation at home.

When the children were 4 years old, their relationship with their mother was once again studied in the home situation and also in a test situation. There were barely any differences beween the stay-at-home children and those in care outside the home, except in obedience. Children in care outside the home were significantly more often disobedient to their mothers than the stay-at-home children. The researchers wondered if the difference in obedience was the result of a greater maturity (following their own will) or whether it was the result of an underlying fear or anger (resistance to the mother). According to them, other research material pointed to the latter interpretation. The mothers of children in care outside the home, for instance, said more often that their children suffered from tantrums and fears.

The researchers can only speculate about the background of these differences. Perhaps the mothers of children in care outside the home feel more need of keeping a hold on their children as a reaction to the motherly fear of the daily separations, and the children resist this. It is also possible that the mothers have been more indulgent, and have not dared to make too many demands on the child as a compensation for their daily absence. The tantrums and disobedience of the 4-year-old children in care outside the home are, according to Rubenstein and Howes, normal for stay-at-home children at the age of 2. Perhaps their development in this area is somewhat delayed, or follows a slightly different course. Perhaps children in care outside the home start the power struggle with their mother at a later age, and attempt later to find out whether they can be somebody with a will of their own, without mother leaving them.

ATTACHMENT THEORY AS A PHILOSOPHY OF CHILD RAISING

The above-mentioned situational analyses are difficult to incorporate into attachment theory as a universal theory of the emotional development of children. The theory is not concerned with the differences in the relationships that children have with adults, but with the way all the 'attachment figures' should behave: responsively, sensitively, making themselves available, so that the child can safely develop attachments. Because of this 'universal' orientation, a number of questions about shared parenthood and child-care outside the home cannot be answered from within this theory.

Another question is: what is wrong with advising parents and teachers to be sensitive and responsive? In my view nothing, and at the same time everything. Nothing, because in our culture trustworthy parents who watch and listen to their child are a highly valued commodity. Everything, because within the attachment theory no insights are given into the specific way in which emotional relationships are regulated between women/mothers, men/fathers and children in our culture. The theory discloses nothing about the way in which the regulation of emotional relationships is associated with questions of power.

The latter becomes clear if attachment theory is read as a philosophy of child raising. Bowlby's theories can be seen as modern variations on the 'maternal love pedagogy' of Pestalozzi and Froebel. In earlier chapters I have shown how, since the Enlightenment, new ways have been sought, on the one hand to free the child from external force and authoritarian (fatherly) authority and, on the other, to restrict and discipline the child. Self-discipline became an important aim of child raising. According to Pestalozzi and Froebel, children develop self-discipline in and through maternal love. Out of love for the mother, the child will resist selfishness. According to Bowlby in the 'maternal deprivation' theory, the mother has to be a 'psychic organizer' and help the child regulate impulses of love and hate. If she does this well, the child will develop a self-regulating ability. If the child is deprived of this maternal love, it will become a danger to society, and when it becomes adult will be controllable only by means of brute force.

In attachment theory, a contradiction is postulated between remaining close and exploratory behaviour. This contradiction can also be overcome with the help of the mother who is sensitive and responsive, who gives the child the feeling of being able to control her behaviour. If he leaves her, he knows she will remain available. In this way, very early on, the gulf is firmly asserted between the *outside world* – school and work – on the one hand, where we are supposed to be independent and self-reliant, and the *inside world* – family and mother – on the other hand, where we expect emotional availability. This emotional regulation is characteristic of our culture. For example, in some African cultures children of 2 years of age are separated quite abruptly from their mothers, and forced to seek protection within child groups (LeVine, 1983).

In order to give the child the feeling of controlling the behaviour of the mother (figure), the power of mothers should remain, as far as possible, *invisible*. According to Stayton, Hogan and Ainsworth (1971), a cooperative mother will not impose her will on her child, but organize her time and the environment in such a way that she will rarely have to disturb or reprimand it. If she has to intervene, she is very clever at 'mood setting', which means that the child will accept her wishes as something he wants as well. A mother's own (career) wishes, activities and thoughts are usually placed in a negative light, as characteristics of a non-sensitive mother. Conceptualized in this fashion, *self-confidence is something received passively by the child, and based on an illusion*; the mother must act as though she has no power. If her power becomes visible it will damage his self-confidence.

In every philosophy of child raising the question of power is raised, explicitly or otherwise, when dealing with obedience and spoiling. According to Bowlby there can be no question of spoiling as long as the needs of the child regulate the attention of the mother (figure). Securely attached children willingly obey their mothers (Stayton, Hogan and Ainsworth, 1971). Anxiously attached children, especially those who are 'avoidance attached' or 'defensive independents', are, by contrast, disobedient, more aggressive and less social. The latter is emphasized by Belsky (1988): child-care outside the home supposedly carries the risk of disobedient, aggressive children.

Insight into *the relation between strong attachment and obedience* is much older than attachment theory. According to Pestalozzi, out of love for the mother the child will abandon the 'passions that make it so unlovable'. Mulder stated in 1827 that the 'pleasant urge for cosiness and contact' and 'timidity' make the child aware of its dependence on God and its parents: because of this, it is educable. Froebel was of the opinion that the child learned about Divine unity and community feeling through maternal love, and would therefore abandon selfishness and crudeness. And, according to psychoanalysts such as Klein and Bettelheim, a deep-rooted fear of separation and loss of love forms a strong motive for children to obey.

Within attachment theory, however, the strong bond is not conceptualized as a starting point for the questions of power between children and their parents. The strong bond is seen as the result of the harmonious interaction and communicative processes between mother and child. On this point Bowlby holds a substantially different opinion from that of the above-mentioned pedagogues and psychoanalysts, who did not place the needs of the child on an equal footing with the right of the child to satisfaction, as did Bowlby. Froebel felt that a well-cared-for child should be left to cry. If this was not done, it would grow up to be a tyrant; the child must learn to bear suffering and pain (Froebel, 1928: 113–14). Psychoanalysts held the view that because of the inherent psychological conflicts, complete satisfaction was not only impossible, but also undesirable. According to Mahler, Pine and Bergman (1980) and Mannoni (1977), the child becomes aware of itself as a person separated from the mother/care-taker only through grief, disappointment and conflicts of will. The child cannot be everything for the mother, just as the mother cannot be everything for the child. The symbiosis is broken and, according to Mahler, the child is 'psychically born' in this process of separation.

Bruno Bettelheim goes a step further. In his view, without a deep fear of their parents children do not give up the 'pleasure principle' (Bettelheim, 1980: 127–41, 169–84). Children who have been brought up 'permissively' are supposedly too easily overwhelmed by frustrated wishes to be able to concentrate on difficult, long-term aims. Besides, child rearers should help children to deal with their own impulses of aggression and violence by commanding, forbidding and setting an example.

Within attachment theory, the psychic conflicts described by the analysts are noticeably absent. There are no conflicts between feelings of love and hate, between wanting to be one and wanting to be separated, between id, ego and superego. And, even if one starts from a less conflict-ridden view of humanity, it remains a fact that reacting 'sensitively' to needs is still a question of interpretation and mutual adaptation.

Parents as well as children make use of their power if things are not going the way they want them to. The power they hold over each other is, to a large extent, drawn from the value they attach to each other and to their emotional bond. In this way, mothers who feel insecure and full of guilt can allow their children to terrorize them. In the case of child abuse by parents, the child can do nothing without the help of a third party; they themselves have no more power than the emotional value they represent. By not exploring the relationships between emotional bonds, discipline and power relationships between parents/ mothers and children, a fundamental moment is missed in the process of child raising.

It is very probably true that in a culture where external force becomes less important, and direct satisfaction of needs more possible thanks to abundant supply, a pedagogy based on attachment relationships and love becomes more important, and that a *love-orientated pedagogy* works best within an intensive personal relationship with one or two child raisers. Bettelheim (1977) pointed out that children who have few contacts other than their mother become very strongly orientated to her. These children learn at a very early age to distinguish even the smallest changes in her voice, her physical attitude and her choice of words. She is their world. Her attention is an absolute necessity of life, in order to avoid the loss of 'self' and loneliness. The mothers of these children very often need not explicitly forbid anything, because subtle forms of disapproval and withdrawal of love are sufficient.

Seen in this context, Bowlby's anxiety about anxiously attached children becomes clear. If children have to watch their mother too much there is no room left for the outside world (the clingers). But if they are not bothered by loss of attention or separation, they become ineducable (the defensive independents). This is the reason why Bowlby sees a connection between an insecure attachment to the mother and criminality. Children who are not concerned enough about their mother's praise stay too far from God, as Mulder put it in 1827.

THE MOTHER AS THERAPIST?

As far as can be seen, Bowlby designed a pedagogy directed towards individuality and independence in the outside world (of men), on the basis of a strong relationship with a direct satisfaction of needs by a mother (figure) who is available at home. This philosophy of child raising is difficult to apply within child-care situations outside the home. But how applicable is it to parents/mothers bringing up their children at home?

Attachment theory is based on the theory of evolution. But if we look at the demands made on the mother (figure), we find they are the same as the demands that can be made on a therapist: absolute availability, sensitivity and responsiveness to the client (or the child). As a psychiatrist, Bowlby was probably successful with his clients. But how realistic is it to model the ideal mother on a psychiatrist? Structurally, the therapeutic situation has different characteristics to the child raising situation. The space given by the therapist to the client, as well as the division of responsibility between client and therapist, are framed within strict rules during a session. Therapists can give the client all their attention because they know that after three-quarters of an hour, or at the most ninety minutes, the client will leave. They can listen understandingly to the client's experiences because they have no responsibility for the client's behaviour. Most therapists cannot keep up this sort of concentrated attention for more than an hour or two per client. But what happens if this behaviour is recommended for situations outside the therapy room?

At home parents and children are dealing with each other day and night. Even the most child-centred parents have household chores or other children to look after. According to Bowlby, mothers should be relieved as much as possible from household work, as this disturbs their real work, the child raising (Bowlby, 1988: 13). But why are children not allowed to know that their parents have other things to do besides looking after them? Why must the power between parents and children remain invisible, thus hiding the fact that the parents bring up their children?

These are old questions that have been posed ever since Rousseau's *Emile*. In 1798, after attempting to bring up their eldest son according to Rousseau's principles, the Edgeworths wrote:

> Rousseau desires, what *we should not let our pupil know is that in doing our will he is obedient to us.* But why? Why should we not let a child know the truth? If we attempt to conceal it, we shall only get into endless absurdities and difficulties.
>
> (*Essays on Practical Education*, 1815: 224, italics in original)

With the rise of 'permissive education' after the Second World War, large groups of middle-class parents once again worried about these questions. According to Sibylle Escalona (1949), parents are given an impossible task if they try to make themselves subordinate to the (developing) needs of their children. Martha Wolfenstein said in 1951 that parents become very unsure of themselves if they have to depend on signals from the children and nuances in their own feelings which are not controllable by voluntary decisions. Van den Berg (1958) felt that compulsory maternal love would degenerate into artificial love, and lead to ambivalence and a suffocating emotional confusion between mother and child.

In their research at the beginning of the sixties, John and Elisabeth Newson (1974) found that middle class mothers were often unable to meet their own ideal of the sensitive, understanding mother. After several abortive attempts to distract their curious 1-year-old from the electric socket, most of them changed to a more direct approach: 'Stop that!', smacking and rages were not unusual phenomena. The women's movement pointed out what a depressing effect a pedagogy can have when it denies or forbids women's own ambitions (Comer, 1974). Philipson (1982) showed in her research how this can lead to mothers living only through their children, and being unable to let go of them. A vague boundary between mother and child is said to lead to 'narcissistic' personalities.

In present-day literature on upbringing and children's development, separation problems as well as discipline problems are only too well known. Different solutions have been offered. Nancy Chodorow (1978) and attachment theoreticians working from the extension hypothesis all plead for shared parenthood (Van IJzendoorn, Tavecchio, Goossens and Vergeer, 1982). By requiring only part-time availability from fathers and mothers, the rest of the time can be used to fulfil other ambitions. All these authors, however, uphold the separation between working outside the home and being available at home, along with the accompanying philosophy of child raising.

Another solution is the cry heard from experts that parents should once again start setting limits. The child asks for limits says the Dutch child psychiatrist Frank Verhulst (1987). The necessity of limits, is argued with reference to the child's needs; parents must once again start bringing up their children. According to Alice Miller (1981, 1983), parents, on the contrary, have in the past brought their children up too strictly, and used them for their own (subconscious) fears and wishes. She is of the opinion that parents must work on a greater consciousness of their own emotional conflicts and defence mechanisms.

All these solutions have in common that the power relations between parents and children are neither thought through nor based on situational analyses of present-day child raising. I will clarify this with an example. On a farm, the daily rhythm and the behaviour of the adults and children used to be determined to a large extent by the character of the business. Children had enough space to play outside but, at the same time, they had to adapt early to adult life. If mother was busy making cheese or butter, it was clear she could pay little attention to the children. The situation of a mother spending the greater part of the day on her own with her children is totally different. If she wants to read the paper, she is going to have to give much more personal reasons for not wanting to pay any attention. She has no social reasons upheld by a social group. She will continually have to decide limits for herself – limits which, because of their individual character, can seem quite arbitrary. Can I expect understanding from a child of this age? Am I too impatient? In a child-rasing situation like this, self-knowledge and an insight into psychological processes are probably very important. But to what extent is Miller's advice realistic for mothers? Should they all go into therapy before the birth of their first child? And the advice to set limits completely ignores the limitlessness in the family, caused by social isolation and by a pedagogy in which household work and the mother's wishes are defined as being contrary to the interest of the child.

The first step in re-thinking this problem must be recognition of the fact that the combination of social isolation of mother and child, strong emotional bonds, and discipline based on manipulation of the emotional bond is a source of uncertainty for the mother about upbringing and the problems of discipline and separation.

In the second place, we have to recognize that, in an isolated family situation, misuse of power by mothers and fathers against their children can remain hidden from the environment for a long time. It is quite probable that the misuse of power is strengthened by *not* talking about power and the (potential) conflicts between parents and children, but seeing harmony as the norm; in this way aggression and power remain taboo.

Thirdly, we must stop maintaining the illusion of the family and the mother acting as a protection against the hostile outside world. It is not the case that the family and the mother offer only love and protection; just as it is not the case that the outside world cannot offer emotional support. Sensitivity and responsiveness are incorrectly placed in opposition to the visible exercise of power.

The children's needs and the needs of the mothers/parents should not be seen as absolute opposites. Experience with the adult world through work inside and outside the home, as well as confrontations with values, standards and rules, are probably very important for children. Into this world the child will eventually grow and in it become adult.

Chapter 9

Conclusions

In earlier chapters I have shown how from the eighteenth century onwards, pedagogues, psychologists and social reformers have dreamed of creating a better society by bringing up young children outside the home and by educating their mothers. I have described international social movements whose aim was to improve child rearing at home by instituting day-care centres and schools for young children. What were the main social and political objectives of these social movements? What theories about the child and the mother or parents were developed and used to support or criticize these social movements? What values and interests were involved?

I tried to analyse the embeddedness of policies as well as pedagogical and psychological theories in shared values, interests and dreams of the future. In this last chapter I will summarize my most important findings.

SOCIAL MOVEMENTS FOR CHILD-CARE OUTSIDE THE HOME

In most social movements, child-care outside the home has been seen as an instrument for reforming child rearing at home in order to create a better society, or in order to regulate sociopolitical conflicts.

In the early nineteenth century, infant schools were heralded as a panacea for the prevention of criminality and 'immorality' in the lower social classes. In the late nineteenth century, Froebel's kindergarten was advocated as an instrument for the elevation of mankind, especially the middle and upper classes, and to prevent criminality in the lower classes and amongst ethnic minorities.

In the early twentieth century, American psychologists and educators discovered the nursery school as a 'laboratory of human relations'. In the nursery schools children were available for scientific observation and for experiments with 'scientific' education, and their mothers for education by the experts. Science promised better-educated human beings.

In the 1960s, child-care centres were rediscovered as an instrument for intervening in the upbringing of small children from the lower social classes and ethnic minorities. Their (supposed) intellectual retardation was to be counteracted by a stimulating environment outside the home. Socio-political conflicts between black and white and between social classes would be moderated by equalizing educational opportunities. In the same period, experts rediscovered child-care centres, the play groups, as a 'finding place' of children and an instrument for the early detection of developmental disturbances and their prevention. Expert guidance promised healthy members of a healthy society. At the same time, feminists of the second wave called for day-care centres as an instrument for achieving equal opportunities and female emancipation.

The most successful social movements, which enjoyed the strongest support from pedagogues and psychologists, have been those which advocated child-care centres for educational objectives (preparation for elementary school and socialization in age groups), and for expert guidance of children and their mothers. For children from the lower classes this was associated with prevention of criminality, immorality and socio-political conflicts. The child had to be removed from the bad family. For the middle and upper classes it was associated with elevating mankind, experimenting with new 'child-centred' methods of child rearing, and raising the status of motherhood.

The least successful movements were those which argued for day-care centres to free the mother from her daily duties. Both the day-care centres for children and mothers/parents in need and those which the feminists called for were, and still are, marginal in the network of provisions for families with young children. Until recently they received very little expert attention, and most of that negative.

The enthusiasm for, and resistance against, child-care outside the home reflects the ambivalent attitude towards mothers' care of small children in the home. On the one hand, it is assumed that mothers cannot properly take care of, socialize and educate their children without expert control and guidance. Children need professional teachers for their socialization in age groups, and for their intellectual development and moral education. At the same time, mothers are held responsible for the emotional well-being of their children. They should be constantly available at home. Child-care outside the family is presented as in the interest of the child, and *not* as an alternative to upbringing within the family or in the interest of working mothers.

Initially, most social movements were not very precise about the age of admission to child-care facilities ('young children' could mean children from 5 years to 1 year of age, or even younger), or about the hours of opening. In practice, however, child-care outside the home was to some degree accepted for 2- and 3-year-olds, and desired for 4- and 5-year-olds. The hours of opening were usually too short to be of help to the children of mothers working outside the family. The most controversial proposal was day-care for babies and toddlers.

Like the ideologies of the social movements, psychological theories – especially those focusing on cognitive and social learning – were initially unclear about the desirable age of admission. Theorists like Mulder and Owen in the nineteenth century and Watson in the twentieth century were against child rearing in the family, and advocated professional rearing for toddlers or even newborn babies. On the other hand, theorists of emotional development such as Winnicott and Bowlby warned of the risks of separating a child from its mother before the age of 3. In practice, theories of emotional development have mostly been used to argue *against* day-care and care outside the home for babies, and theories about social and cognitive learning to argue for other forms of child-care outside the home.

In short, in the practice of child-care outside the family and the associated pedagogic and psychological theories, the following values and interests have been fostered: child rearing at home, prevention of conflicts between the social classes, the superiority of expert knowledge and an available mother as secure base for the child's entry into society.

SCIENCE AND CHILD REARING

The attitude of pedagogues and psychologists towards child-care outside the home has its roots, to a large extent, in the philosophical attitudes of the Enlightenment towards the controllability of human development. According to Locke, Owen and the twentieth-century behaviourists, man could to a large extent be moulded, if use was made of scientific knowledge of the laws governing human learning.

Froebel, Stanley Hall and Gesell were convinced that children's natural development was predetermined, but that scientific observation could discover and prevent any 'abnormalities'. During the fifties, psychoanalysts such as Winnicott and Bowlby were of the opinion that the (irrational) emotional nature of children could be channelled in the right direction with the help of scientific insight. In spite of their differences, all these theoreticians have in common a conviction that application of scientific knowledge will make for better human beings.

The optimistic believers in the power of knowledge had their drawbacks for mothers and children. The educator/mother became the mediator between the potential in the child and the ideal society. Therefore, mothers were idealized, but simultaneously blamed for the evils of society. At the same time, since mothers were lay persons, they needed expert knowledge and guidance.

In the light of this claim to superiority by the scientists it becomes clear why some forms of child-care centres were welcomed. The nursery schools were a playground for scientific observations and experiments, and intended to guide middle-class mothers scientifically. Among Head Start child-care centres a scientifically grounded form of care was offered to children who were disadvantaged at home. Child-care centres were valued as places where children could be scientifically studied, and as an instrument of passing on scientific knowledge to mothers, and applying it to disadvantaged children.

The scientists' negative attitude towards child-care centres also has its roots in Enlightenment philosophy: in the relation posited between love and discipline. Ever since the Enlightenment, pedagogues and psychologists have endeavoured to free the child's nature from external authority and tradition. The emphasis on 'freedom' in no way means that these theoreticians were advocates of absolute freedom for the child. Quite the opposite. They sought 'rational sanctions' for limiting its freedom and fostering self-discipline. The relation between freedom and commitment became a real problem.

Pedagogues like Pestalozzi and Froebel and psychologists like Winnicott and Bowlby sought the solution to this problem in the emotional bond between the mother and child. As early as 1827, Mulder wrote that the 'instinct towards togetherness' and 'fear of separation' make the child compliant. Harsh discipline should be replaced by love-orientated discipline or maternal sensitivity and availability. During the 1950s it was hypothesized that separation from the mother and/or maternal insensitivity caused criminality and (incurable) mental disturbances.

These theories do not only reinforce the value of child-rearing at home; they also sanction the split between the domain of paid work or the outside world on the one hand, and the domain of the home on the other. In the proposed regulation of emotional and moral life, the mother should figure as a secure base from which the child (and the husband) can explore the 'strange' and 'dangerous' outside world. In order for the child to feel safe, the mother has to be devoid of needs of her own. Against this background, the negative reactions to day-care and the working mother are understandable: deep-rooted values and power relations between men and women, and between the generations, are threatened.

Theoreticians who advocated child-care centres, such as Owen and Watson, wanted nothing to do with 'irrational' emotions. They argued for a 'rational scientific approach', and emphasized social learning and cognition. (Consider the 'habit training programmes' in the nursery schools, and the compensation programmes within Project Head Start.) It was very much easier for the theoreticians of learning to feel themselves superior to mothers/parents than for the theoreticians in the emotional field.

AMBIVALENCE IN FEMINISM

In the literature on child-care outside the home, there are three characteristic attitudes to mothers: glorification, the urge to improve and exploitation. But women have not been passive victims of these attitudes; on the contrary. Feminists in the nineteenth century associated the gospel of the new 'child-centred' education with the sanctity of motherhood, and with their right to academic education and paid jobs in the kindergartens. Academically trained mothers in nursery schools and play groups were concerned with professionalizing motherhood and reconstructing education around the 'natural' development of the child. Our century has numbered many famous female peda- gogues and developmental psychologists.

At first sight, the call for day-care centres by feminists of the second wave contradicts the 'women's mission' of the kinder- garten movement and the 'child-centred' motives of the mothers in the play-group movement. But in this study I have hypothe- sized that both feminist attitudes towards motherhood spring from common historical origins. They were both rooted in the split between the domain of paid work and the domain of the home, and in the rise of new 'enlightened' ideas of reforming mankind by education.

Feminists in the nineteenth century accepted their feminine role. The kindergarten movement, with its mission of human- izing mankind by means of an enlightened education of children, tried to open up the constricted life-space of the home. Feminists of the second wave, in contrast, rebelled against their feminine role and the split between the world of paid work and the family. They wanted it both ways: being a mother *and* having equal chances on the labour market. Enlightenment ideas about the changeability of mankind were used to legitimize their rights as women.

Women in both traditions of feminism were forced to discover that the care of young children is valued in words and feelings, but that society refuses to take responsibility for it in the form of well-paid jobs and academic status for kindergarten teachers (in the nineteenth century), or sufficient high-quality day-care pro- visions for children of working mothers (in our time). Caring for children is undervalued women's work.

THE INVENTION OF 'THE CHILD' AND 'THE MOTHER'

The split between the domain of paid work and the home, caused by complex processes of industrialization and urbanization, also had far-reaching consequences for the lives of children. Sociali- zation and the transmission of knowledge through day-to-day contact with working grown-ups became problematic, especially for boys. The school was invented to educate and discipline the children. Infant schools and kindergartens had to bridge the gap between home and school. The school and child-care centre can be seen as symbols of the 'child's world' in our culture. These 'child's worlds' had to be filled up. What should be done with fifty, 100 or even 400 small children packed together in one room? It took more than a century before 'child-centred' pedagogy was invented for the child-care centres, pre-schools, and the living rooms or nurseries in middle-class families with their doll's houses, puzzles, construction kits and so on.

Froebel was the first pedagogue to design a curriculum based on the 'natural' development of the child. The kindergarten teacher had to model herself after his idealized image of the mother totally devoted to her child. But in reality, it was the kindergarten teacher who worked in a 'child's world', without household chores or other obligations, and who was trained in child rearing. And so the idealized kindergarten teacher became the model for the good mother. At a theoretical level the mother's household chores and other obligations disappeared, or were transformed into (potentially) pedagogic games for the children. In most middle-class families with children we can now find a corner or a room for children with dolls, bricks and other developmental material.

The creation of this socially empty space for children also had far-reaching consequences for the sort of educational aims the parents sought. Previously, children had been brought up to be farmers, bakers, seamstresses or housewives. Nowadays, children are brought up to be flexible employees; they must 'learn to learn'. The development of the child becomes, in itself, an aim. Child psychologists filled the emptiness created by the disappearance of concrete social goals with standards for 'normal' development in physical, cognitive, emotional and moral fields. The social and personal meaning of behaviour – does he like butterflies? does she help her father and mother well? – receded into the background, in order to make way for scores on development charts.

The activities of observing, measuring and judging children on the basis of knowledge of developmental psychology were brought to parents by the health clinics and by literature on education and child rearing. In this area, a second curious circularity can be seen between the image of the child-rearing experts and that of the parents/mothers. As one of the first child psychologists, G. Stanley Hall, used parents/mothers as a source of information on children. But very soon, this source of information was discarded as being 'laymen's knowledge' and therefore of inferior value. Good mothers had to learn to watch their child more objectively. In this way *the scientist became the model for the ideal mother.*

In the case of morality, the same disappearance of the socially meaningful aims of child rearing took place. An abstract internalized morality has become more important than the transmission of clear images of what may or may not be done. An abstract morality was connected to a close bond between mother/parent and child. The mother must be sensitive towards her child to enable a close bond to grow, but at the same time give the child space to explore. In the twentieth century, this image of the mother has arisen from psychoanalytical and therapeutic literature. It is the image of the ideal mother created by therapists and based on their work with patients. Because therapists, due to the nature of their work, were able to be completely available and sensitive to the feelings and signals of their patients during a therapeutic session, they were much better able to meet the demands of the ideal mother than were real mothers at home. Thus, *the therapist became the model for the ideal mother.*

Experts on upbringing have gained their knowledge of children in situations where children, to a large extent, were cut off from broader social relations and contacts: the classroom, the research laboratory, the consulting room. Because of this, on the one hand they have confirmed an image of 'the development' of 'the child' without a social context. On the other hand, through their knowledge, techniques of upbringing and child-centred pedagogy, they have filled up the social void in which the children had landed. For mothers this meant that their work, interests and responsibilities apart from their children were denied. The mother and her young child were bound together. Not only that: mothers also had to mould themselves on images of child-rearing experts: the scientist, the teacher, the therapist. Is it surprising that nowadays there are so many complaints about mothers' uncertainty about child rearing?

BREAKING FREE FROM THE 'CHILD-CENTRED' DISCOURSE

Bringing up young children is subject to change. Mothers working outside the home have become more accepted, and there will probably be more provisions made for child-care facilities. At the present time, child psychologists are arguing for a broader upbringing; the value of the father and other care takers is receiving more attention. But my argument in this study is that more needs to be done. The foundations on which the current policy and scientific research into young children are based are in need of a change. In the first place, the idea of the family round which the policies and scientific research are centred, and which presupposes that one parent/mother is available and responsible for the daily care and the other parent/father is responsible for earning a family income, must be changed. This presupposition does not coincide with the present situation in which many parents want to combine paid work with the care of children.

In the second place, the Utopian philosophy surrounding children and their upbringing must be modified. A better society cannot be achieved purely by changing child rearing. It is questionable to what extent the development of children is controllable, not only because of the children's own contribution, but also because many external influences are outside the reach of the care-giver, such as television, commercialization and living conditions. The different 'temperaments' with which children are born probably also have a large influence. Parents and others involved can offer the child all sorts of opportunities, and they can also do a great deal of damage.

However, psychologists like Piaget and psychoanalysts such as Mannoni and Bettelheim are, in my view, correct when they draw attention to the mental and physical strength with which children create an image of themselves and the world. Children develop their own strategies – whether these are called defences, inventions or fantasies – to solve conflicts and problems or make them manageable, and their own theories in order to understand the world. Very often, these strategies and theories are much more realistic than they at first appear to adults. From longitudinal research it appears that the development of children at a later age is not predictable from early experiences, not only because children do different things with their experiences, but also because later situations can impede the possibilities of 'working through'. Survival strategies born from necessity can be useful in later situations, but the opposite can also be the case.

Parents/mothers, therefore, cannot be held solely responsible for the adult who grows from the child. Large intervention programmes such as Head Start should not be judged in the first place on their long-term effects on goals which may be a long way from those of the children and parents involved, such as the lessening of social injustice between the social classes. It is incorrect to see children only as future adults, or instruments for a better society. An improvement of the quality of life and better chances in the short term should be sufficient goals. Problems such as lack of space for children on the street, poverty, discrimination and inequality should be looked into in other places and at different levels: not only within the family and child rearing, but within trade and industry, politics and policies. An educational aim which is too high, and thus not achieved, inevitably backfires on the intended group: the object of the desire for improvement (mothers and/or children) are blamed for the failure of the intervention.

In the third place, the philosphy of the development of 'the child' must be reviewed. This philosophy completely ignores the power relations between the sexes, classes, ethnic groups and generations. These power relations cannot be broken solely by child rearing, but they can be reflected upon in research, and this, in turn, may offer new perspectives on old problems. Situational models will have to be developed which correctly reflect the consequences of these power relations for children, parents and others involved with children. At the present time, experts on upbringing – scientists, teachers and therapists – all project their own knowledge and situations onto the parents/mothers. For this reason, they are not only in danger of offering impractical advice to parents, but, because of their claim to superiority, they can also undermine the self-confidence of parents and others involved. There must be more respect for the knowledge obtained from and about children from different perspectives and backgrounds of experience.

In Chapter 8 I put forward a proposal for a situational analysis of present-day family upbringing of young children, and the often-heard complaints about uncertainty in child rearing, and problems surrounding separation and discipline. In my opinion, the complaints are associated with a 'child-centred' pedagogy, in which children and their mothers are isolated from broader social connections, and in which child rearing has become the invisible exercise of power, unrelated to adults' work. The rules and limits mothers have to place on their children within the family situation are very often individual and arbitrary, because they are not upheld by a broader social group. Think only of the difference between the mother reading the newspaper, who has to give a personal reason why she cannot pay the child any attention, and the farmer's wife making cheese, with others. The confusion about what mother wants and what the child wants, and the possibilities of escalation – mothers who are unable to set any limits, and anger and tantrums – are strengthened by a pedagogic philosophy in which mothers' work in the house is totally ignored or degraded to 'child's play', and in which the exercise of power has become invisible. All this undermines the position of mothers as adult women.

The exercise of power has become invisible in three ways. According to the 'child-centred' pedagogy, it has to be largely invisible and exercised through bonds of love and diversion of attention. The misuse of power within families remains invisible to the outside world for too long, leaving the child in an extremely vulnerable position. The power that parents and children have and use so as to give their life form is seen too little, and is negatively valued if their life style diverges too much from the experts' ideal. As an example of the latter we only have to think of the negative reactions from experts on child rearing to the efforts made by women to combine work outside the home with their care for the children.

This problem cannot be solved by fathers 'mothering', and by quantitative expansion of child-care facilities for the children of mothers working outside the home. It is not unthinkable that within a couple of decades, fathers will develop the same uncertainty in child rearing now shown by mothers. And mothers will become overburdened because the demands made by a 'child-centred' upbringing are not changed, and in their employment too little account is taken of the home situation. It is also just as important to consider what joint responsibility for the care of children could mean at different levels of society.

We will have to create a new 'in-between area' to bridge the gulf that has developed in industrialized society between the outside world and the family.

References

Addams, J. (1910) *Twenty Years at Hull House*, New York.

Adorno, T.W., Frenkel-Brunswick, E.F. Levinson, D.J. and R. Nevitt Sanford (1990) *The Authoritarian Personality*, Norwood, New York.

Ainsworth, M.D.S. and S.M. Bell (1974) Mother–infant interactions and the development of competence. In: *The Growth of Competence*, K. Connolly and J. Bruner (eds), London.

Ainsworth, M.D.S., Bell, S.M.V. and D.J. Stayton (1971) Individual differences in strange-situation behaviour of one-year olds. In: *The Origins of Human Social Relations*, H.R. Schaffer (ed.), London.

Ainsworth, M.D.S., Blehar, M.C., Waters, E. and S. Walls (1978) *Patterns of Attachment: A Psychological Study of the Strange Situation*, Hillsdale, NJ.

Anderson, J. (1956) Child development: an historical perspective. In: *Child Development* 27: 181–96.

Anderson, J.E. (1946) Methods of child psychology. In: *Manual of Child Psychology*, L. Carmichael (ed.), New York.

Arrington, R.E. (1943) Time sampling in studies of social behaviour: a critical review of techniques and results with research suggestions. In: *Psychological Bulletin* 40: 81–124.

As the twig is bent . . .Lasting effects of preschool programs (1983) The Consortium for Longitudinal Studies, LEA, Hillsdale, NJ.

Badinter, E. (1981) *The Myth of Motherhood: An Historical View of the Maternal Instinct*, London.

Barglow, P., Vaughn, B. and N. Molitor (1987) Effects of maternal absence due to employment on the quality of infant–mother attachment in a low-risk sample. In: *Child Development* 58: 945–54.

Baruch, H.E. (1937) A study of reported tensions in interparental relationships as coexistent with behaviour adjustment in young children. In: *Journal of Experimental Child Psychology* 6: 187–204.

Bee, H.L., Egeren, L.F., Streissguth, A.P., Nyman, B.A. and M.S. Leckie (1969) Social class differences in maternal teaching strategies and speech patterns. In: *Developmental Psychology* 1: 726–34.

Beller, K. (1985) Early intervention programs. In: *Handbook of Infant Development*, J. Osofsky (ed.), J. Wiley & Son, New York.

Belsky, J. (1988) The 'effects' of infant day care reconsidered. In: *Early Childhood Research Quarterly* 3: 235–72.

Belsky, J. and L.D. Steinberg (1978) The effects of day care: a critical review. In: *Child Development* 49: 929–49.

Belsky, J. and M.J. Rovine (1988) Nonmaternal care in the first year of life and the security of infant–parent attachment. In: *Child Development* 59: 157–67.

Bender, L. and H. Yarnell (1941) An observation nursery. In: *American Journal of Psychiatry* 97: 1158–67.

Benn, R.K. (1986) Factors promoting secure attachment relationships between employed mothers and their sons. In: *Child Development* 57: 1224–31.

Berdenis van Berlekom, I.I. (1842) *Beknopt geschiedkundig overzicht der Bewaarscholen*, Middelburg.

Berg, J.H. van den (1958) *Dubieuze liefde in de omgang met het kind*, Nijkerk.

Bettelheim, B. (1977) *The Children of the Dream: Communal Child-rearing and its Implications for Society.* Frogmore, St Albans (first published 1969).

—— (1980) *Surviving*, New York.

Bie, T. de and W. Fritschy (1985) De 'wereld' van Reveilvrouwen. In: *De eerste feministische golf*, J. Reys, T. van Loosbroek, U. Jansz, M. Henneman, A. de Wildt and M. Elias (eds), Nijmegen.

Blanchard, M. and M. Main (1979) Avoidance of the attachment figure and social-emotional adjustment in day-care infants. In: *Developmental Psychology* 15: 445–6.

Blehar, M. Curtis (1974) Anxious attachment and defensive reactions associated with day care. In: *Child Development* 45: 683–92.

Bloch, J.H. (1974) Rousseau's reputation as an authority on childcare and physical education in France before the revolution. In: *Pedagogica Historica* XIV, Gent 5–33.

Block, R.H. (1978) Ideals of Transition. The rise of the moral mother, 1785–1815. In: *Feminist Studies* 4: 101–26.

Bloom, B.S. (1966) *Stability and Change in Human Characteristics*, John Wiley, New York.

Borstelman, L.J. (1974) Classics in developmental psychology: historical persons and studies in common textbook references. In: *Developmental Psychology* 10: 661–4.

—— (1983) Children before psychology: ideas about children from antiquity to the late 1800s. In: *Handbook of Child Psychology*, P.H. Mussen (ed.), 4th edition, vol. I, *History, Theory, and Methods*, W. Kessen (vol. ed.), New York.

Bowlby, J. (1952) *Maternal Care and Mental Health*, World Health Organization, Geneva (first published 1951).

—— (1978a) *Attachment and Loss*, vol. 1, *Attachment*, Harmondsworth (1971).

—— (1978b) *Attachment and Loss*, vol. 2, *Separation: Anxiety and Anger*, Harmondsworth (1973).

—— (1979a) *The Making and Breaking of Affectional Bonds*, London.

—— (1979b) Psychoanalysis and child care (1956). In: J. Bowlby, *The*

Making and Breaking of Affectional Bonds, London.

—— (1979c) Child care and the growth of love (1953). In: J. Bowlby, *The Making and Breaking of Affectional Bonds*, London.

—— (1988) *A Secure Base: Clinical Applications of Attachment Theory*, London.

Bowles, S. and H. Gintis (1976) *Schooling in Capitalist America: Educational Reform and the Contradictions of Economic Life*, Routledge and Kegan Paul, London.

Bradbord, M. and R. Endsley (1980) The importance of educating parents to be discriminating day care consumers. In: *Advances in Early Education and Day Care*, vol. 1, S. Kilmer (ed.), Greenwich, Conn.

Bradbury, D.E. (1939) The contribution of the child study movement to child psychology. In: *Psychological Bulletin* 34: 21–38.

Bronfenbrenner, U. (1975) Is early intervention effective? In: *Handbook of Evaluation Research*, M. Guttentag and E.L. Struening (eds), Sage, Beverly Hills.

—— (1979) *The Ecology of Human Development*. Harvard University Press, Cambridge, Mass.

Bühler, C. (1933) The social behaviour of the child. In: *Handbook of Child Psychology*, C. Murchison (ed.), Worcester, Mass. (first published 1931).

Cable, M. (1972) *The Little Darlings: A History of Child Rearing in America*, New York.

Cairns, R.B. (1983) The emergence of developmental psychology. In: *Handbook of Child Psychology*. Formerly *Carmichael's Manual of Child Development*, P.H. Mussen (ed.), 4th edition, vol. 1, *History, Theory and Methods*, W. Kessen (ed.), New York.

Calcar, E. van (1861) *Onze ontwikkeling of de magt der eerste indrukken*, Amsterdam.

—— (1910) *Frederik Fröbel*, Amsterdam (1879).

—— (1898) *Kindertuin en Moederschool. Openingsrede tot den opvoedkundigen cursus*, The Hague.

Caldwell, B. and J.B. Richmond (1964) Programmed day care for the very young child – a preliminary report. In: *Journal of Marriage and the Family* Nov.: 481–8.

Caldwell, B.M. (1968) The optimal learning environment for the young child. In: *Early Learning and Early Experience*, W. Sluckin (ed.), Harmondsworth.

Casler, L. (1961) Maternal deprivation: a critical review of the literature, *Monograph of Social Research and Child Development* 26: 1–64.

Cavallo, D. (1976) From perfection to habit: moral training in the American kindergarten, 1860–1920. In: *History of Education Quarterly* 16: 147–62.

—— (1979) The politics of latency: kindergarten pedagogy 1860–1930. In: *Regulated Children – Liberated Children*, B. Finkelstein (ed.), New York.

Changing the Subject: Psychology, Social Regulation and Subjectivity, J. Henriques *et al.* (eds), London/New York 1984.

Chess, S. and A. Thomas (1982) Infant bonding: mystique and reality. In: *American Journal of Orthopsychiatry* 52: 213–22.

Chilman, C.S. (1973) Programs for disadvantaged parents: some major trends and related research. In: *Review of Child Development Research* III, B.M. Caldwell, H.N. Ricciuti (eds), Chicago.

Chodorow, N. (1978) *The Reproduction of Mothering: Psychoanalysis and the Sociology of Gender*, Berkeley, Cal.

Clarke, A.M. and A.D.B. Clarke (1976) *Early Experience: Myth and Evidence*, London.

Clarke, K. (1985) Public and private children: infant education in the 1820s and 1830s. In: *Language, Gender and Childhood*, C. Steedman, C. Urwin and V. Walkerdine (eds), London.

Clarke-Stewart, A. (1977) *Child Care in the Family, a Review of Research and Some Propositions for Policy*, New York.

—— (1982) *Day Care*, Glasgow.

—— (1988) 'The "effects" of infant day care reconsidered' reconsidered: risks for parents, children, and researchers. In: *Early Childhood Research Quarterly* 3: 292–318.

—— (1989) Infant day care: maligned or malignant? In: *American Psychologist* 44: 266–73.

Clarke-Stewart, A.K. and G. Fein (1973) *Day Care in Context*, New York.

Clarke-Stewart, A.K. and G.G. Fein (1983) Early childhood programs. In: *Handbook of Child Psychology*. Formerly *Carmichael's Manual of Child Psychology*, P.H. Mussen (ed.), vol. 2, *Infancy and Developmental Psychology*, M.M. Haith and J.J. Campes (eds), John Wiley & Sons, New York.

Clerkx, L.E. (1984) De afstoting van de bewaarfunktie uit het kleuteronderwijs. In: *Comenius* 13: 3–24.

—— (1985) Kinderen in het gezin. In: *Gezinsgeschiedenis*. Vier eeuwen gezin in Nederland, G.A. Kooy (ed.), Assen.

Cohen, S. (1983) The mental hygiene movement, the development of personality and the school: the medicalization of American education. In: *History of Education Quarterly* 23: 123–47.

Comenius, J.A. (1963) *Informatorium der Mutterschule*, Heidelberg (1630).

Comer, L. (1974) *Wedlocked Women*, Feminist Books, Leeds.

Cornelius, S.W. and N.W. Denney (1975) Dependency in day-care and home-care children. In: *Developmental Psychology* 11: 575–82.

Coronel, S. (1864) *De bewaarschool. Haar verleden, tegenwoordige toestand en hare toekomst*, Amsterdam.

Cott, N.F. (1977) *The Bonds of Womanhood: 'Woman's Sphere' in New England 1780–1835*, New Haven, Conn.

Cremin, L.A. (1962) *The Transformation of the School: Progressivism in American Education, 1876–1957*, New York.

Cummings, E.M. (1980) Caregiver stability and day care. In: *Developmental Psychology* 16: 31–7.

Curti, M. (1961) *The Social Ideas of American Educators*, Paterson, NJ.

Datta, L.E. (1979) Another spring and other hopes: some findings from national evaluations of Project Head Start. In: *Project Head Start, a Legacy of the War on Poverty*, E. Zigler and J. Valentine (eds), The Free Press, New York.

Davidson, F., Gornicki, B., International Labour Office, Lebovici, S.,

Lezine, I., Richmond, J.B., Schmidt-Kolmer, E. and S. Sjölin (1964) *Care of Children in Day Centers*, World Health Organization, Geneva.

Davin, A. (1983) *Imperialisme en Moederschapscultus*, KUN, Nijmegen.

Davis, M.D. (1933) *Nursery Schools: their Development and Current Practices in the United States*, Washington, DC.

Dennis, W. (1949) Historical beginnings of child psychology. In: *Psychological Bulletin* 46: 224–35.

Dewey, J. (1899) *The School and Society*. In: J. Dewey, *The Child and the Curriculum and the School and Society*, University of Chicago Press, Chicago.

—— (1903) Foreword. In: *The Psychology of Child Development*, Chicago.

—— (1916) *Democracy and Education*, New York.

Dewey, J. and E. Dewey (1967) *Schools of Tomorrow*, New York.

Diehl, L.A. (1986) The paradox of G. Stanley Hall: foe of coeducation and education of women. In: *American Psychologist* 41: 868–78.

Dietrich, D. and D. Tiedeman (1976) Child psychologist in the eighteenth century. In: *The Historian* 38: 455–73.

Donzelot, J. (1980) *The Policing of Families*, London.

Draijer, N. (1988) *Een lege plek in mijn geheugen: seksueel misbruik van meisjes door verwanten*, The Hague.

Dunn, J. and C. Kendrick (1982) *Siblings: Love, Envy and Understanding*, London.

Easterbrook, M.A. and W.A. Goldberg (1985) Effects of early maternal employment on toddlers, mothers, and fathers. In: *Developmental Psychology* 21: 774–83.

Edgeworth, M. and R.L. Edgeworth (1815) *Essays on Practical Education*, vols I and II, London (1798).

Ehrenreich, B. and D. English (1979) *For Her Own Good: 150 Years of the Expert's Advice to Women*, London.

Erikson, E.H. (1970) *Childhood and Society*, Harmondsworth (1950).

Escalona, S. (1949) A commentary upon some recent changes in child rearing practices. In: *Child Development* 20: 157–62.

Essen, M. van (1985) *Onderwijzeressen in niemandsland*, Nijkerk.

Eysenck, H.J. (1975) Foreword. In: P. Morgan, *Childcare: Sense and Fable*. London.

Farron, D.C. and C.T. Ramey (1977) Infant day care and attachment behaviours toward mothers and teachers. In: *Child Development* 48: 1112–16.

Fein, G.G. (1980) The informed parent. In: *Advances in Early Education and Day Care*, vol. I, S. Kilmer (ed.), Greenwich, Conn.

Fein, G.G. and N. Fox (1988) Infant day care: a special issue. In: *Early Childhood Research Quarterly* 3: 227–34.

Feinstein, K.W. (1979) Directions for day care. In: *Working Women and Families*, Beverly Hills/London.

—— (1980) Kindergartens, feminism, and the professionalization of motherhood. In: *International Journal of Women's Studies* (Canada) 3: 28–38.

FNV-enquete (bedrijfs)kinderopvang in Nederland 1989 (1989) FNV, Amsterdam.

Forest, I. (1929) *Preschool Education: A Historical and Critical Study*, New York.

Foucault, M. (1967) *Madness and Civilisation*, Tavistock, London.

—— (1979) *Discipline and Punishment*, Harmondsworth.

Frank, L.K. (1962) The beginnings of child development and family life education in the twentieth century. In: *Merill-Palmer Quarterly* 8: 207–28.

Freud, A. and S. Dann (1968) An experiment in group upbringing (1951). In: A. Freud, *Indications for Child Analysis and Other Papers*, New York.

Friedan, B. (1963) *The Feminine Mystique*, New York.

Froebel's opvoeding van den Mensch, (1928) vertaald door J.M. Telders, Groningen (first published 1826).

Froebel: uit en over, (1922) inleiding en vertaling opstellen Froebel door J.M. Telders, Zeist (first published 1840).

Gathorne-Hardy, J. (1972) *The Rise and Fall of the British Nanny*, London.

Gesell, A. (1940) *The First Five Years of Life: A Guide to the Study of the Preschool Child*, New York.

Gesell, A. and F. L. Ing (1943) *Infant and Child in the Culture of Today: The Guidance of Development in Home and Nursery School*, New York.

Ginsburg, H. (1972) *The Myth of the Deprived Child: Poor Children's Intellect and Education*, London.

Goossens, F.A. (1986) *Quality of Attachment in Children of Working and Non-working Mothers*, Leuven.

Gordon, E.W. (1979) Evaluation during the early years of Head Start. In: *Project Head Start, a Legacy of the War on Poverty*, E. Zigler and J. Valentine (eds), The Free Press, New York.

Graebner, W. (1980) The unstable world of Benjamin Spock: social engineering in a democratic culture, 1917–1950. In: *The Journal of American History* 67: 612–29.

Grant, E. (1939) The effect of certain factors in the home environment upon child behaviour. In: *University of Iowa Studies in Child Welfare* 15: 61–94.

Gray, S.W. and L.P. Wandersman (1980) The methodology of home-based intervention studies: problems and promising strategies. In: *Child Development* 51: 993–1009.

Grotberg, E.H. (1980) The roles of the federal government in regulation and maintenance of quality in childcare. In: *Advances in Early Education and Day Care*, vol. I, S. Kilmer (ed.), Greenwich, Conn.

Grubb, N.W. and M. Lazerson (1982) *Broken Promises: How Americans Fail their Children*, New York.

Hadow Report (1933) *Report of the Consultative Committee on Infant and Nursery Schools*, HMSO, London.

Hale, N.G. (1971) *Freud and the Americans: The Beginning of Psychoanalysis in the United States, 1876–1917*, New York.

Hall, C. (1985) Private persons versus public someones: class, gender and politics in England, 1780–1850. In: *Language, Gender and Childhood*, C. Steedman, C. Urwin and V. Walkerdine (eds), London.

Hall, Stanley G. (1921) *Aspects of Child Life and Education*, New York (first published 1907).

—— (1928) The Contents of Children's Minds. In: *Aspects of Child Life and Education*, G. Stanley Hall *et al.*, New York (first published 1907).

—— (1974) The ideal school as based on child study (1901). In: *Education in the United States, A Documentary History*, S. Cohen (ed.), vol. III, New York.

Hardyman, C. (1983) *Dream Babies: Child Care from Locke to Spock*, London.

Harrison, J.F.C. (1968) *Robert Owen and the Owenites in Britain and America: The Quest for the New Moral World*, London.

Hattwick, B.W. (1936) Interrelations between the preschool child's behavior and certain factors in the home. In: *Child Development* 7: 200–26.

Hess, R.D., Price, G.G., Dickson, W.P. and M. Conroy (1981) Different roles for mothers and teachers: contrasting styles of child care. In: *Advances in Early Education and Day Care*, vol. II, S. Kilmer (ed.), Greenwich, Conn.

Hesse, S.J. (1979) Women working: historical trends. In: *Working Women and Families*, K.W. Feinstein (ed.), Beverly Hills/London.

Hilgard, E.R. (1957) Freud and experimental psychology. In: *Behavioral Science* 2: 74–9.

Hochschild, A. (1989) *The Second Shift. Working Parents and the Revolution at Home*, Viking Press, New York.

Hock, E. (1978) Working and non working mothers with infants: perceptions of their careers, their infants needs, and satisfaction with mothering. In: *Developmental Psychology* 14: 37–43.

—— (1980) Working and non working mothers and their infants: a comparative study of maternal caregiving characteristics and infant social behavior. In: *Merrill-Palmer Quarterly* 26: 79–101.

Hoffman, L.W. (1974) Effects of maternal employment on the child – a review of the research. In: *Developmental Psychology* 10: 204–28.

—— (1979) Maternal employment, 1979. In: *American Psychologist* 341: 859–65.

Honig, A.S. (1982) Parent involvement in early childhood education. In: *Handbook of Research in Early Childhood Education*, Bernard Spodek (ed.), The Free Press, New York.

Horowitz, F.D. and L.Y. Paden (1973) The effectiveness of environmental intervention programs. In: *Review of Child Development Research*, vol. III, B.M. Caldwell and H.N. Riciutti (eds), Chicago.

Hunt, J. McV. (1961) *Intelligence and Experience*, New York.

Iets ter aanprijzing van bewaarscholen en derzelver algemene verspreiding (1842) Nijmegen.

IJzendoorn, M.H. van and P.M. Kroonenberg (1988) Cross-cultural patterns of attachment: a meta-analysis of the strange situation. In: *Child Development* 59: 147–56.

IJzendoorn, M.H. van and L.W.C. Tavecchio (1987) The development of attachment theory as a Lakatosian research program: philosophical and methodological aspects. In: *Attachment in Social Networks*, L.W.C. Tavecchio and M.H. van IJzendoorn (eds), Amsterdam.

IJzendoorn, M.H. van, Tavecchio, L.W.C., Goossens, F.A. and M.M.

Vergeer (1982) *Opvoeden in geborgenheid: een kritische analyse van Bowlby's attachmenttheorie*, Van Loghum Slaterus, Deventer.

Ingleby, D. (1986) Development in Social Context. In: *Children of Social Worlds*, M. Richards and P. Light (eds), Cambridge.

Isaacs, S. (ed.) (1941) *The Cambridge Evacuation Survey*, London.

—— (1964) *Social Development in Young Children*, London (first published 1933).

Jackson, B. and S. Jackson (1979) *Childminder*, Harmondsworth.

Jacobsen, J. and D. Wille (1984) Influence of attachment and separation experience on separation distress at 18 months. In: *Developmental Psychology* 20: 477–84.

Jensen, A.R. (1969) How much can we boost IQ and scholastic achievement? In: *Harvard Educational Review* 39: 1–123.

Jersild, A.T. (1947) *Child Psychology*, 3rd edition, New York.

Jester, E.R. and B.J. Guinagh (1983) The Gordon Parent Education Infant and Toddler Program. In: *As the twig is bent* . . ., The Consortium for Longitudinal Studies, LEA, Hillsdale, NJ.

Jones, K. and K. Williamson (1979) The birth of the schoolroom. In: *Ideology & Consciousness* 6: 59–110.

Kagan, J., Kearsley, R.B. and P.R. Zelazo (1977) The effects of infant day care on psychological development. In: *Evaluation Quarterly* 1: 109–42.

Kamerman, S.B. and A.J. Kahn (1981) *Child Care, Family Benefits, and Working Parents: a Study in Comparative Policy*, Columbia University Press, New York.

Kamin, L.J. (1977) *The Science and Politics of IQ*, Penguin, Harmondsworth.

Katz, L.G. (1980) Mothering and teaching: some significant distinctions. In: *Current Topics in Early Childhood*, vol. III, L.G. Katz (ed.), Norwood, NJ.

Kemsies, F. (1902) Die Entwicklung der Pädagogischen Psychologie im 19. Jahrhundert. In: *Zeitschrift für Pädagogische Psychologie, Pathologie und Hygiene* 4: 197–211.

Kerr, V. (1973) One step forward – two steps back: child care's long American history. In: *Child Care – Who Cares*, P. Roby (ed.), New York.

Kessel, F.S. and A.W. Siegel (eds) (1981) *The Child and Other Cultural Inventions*, Houston Symposium, no. 4, New York.

Kessen, W. (1965) *The Child*, New York.

—— (1978) Rousseau's children. In: *Daedalus* 107: 155–66.

—— (1983) The American child and other cultural inventions. In: *The Child and Other Cultural Inventions*, F. Kessel and A. Siegel (eds), Houston Symposium, no. 4, New York.

Kilmer, S. (1979) Infant-toddler group day care: a review of research. In: *Current Topics in Early Childhood Education*, vol. II, L.G. Katz (ed.), Abley Publishing Corp., Norwood, NJ.

Kinderopvang en Arbeidsparticipatie van Vrouwen (1987) Ministerie van Sociale Zaken en Werkgelegenheid, The Hague.

Klein, M. (1975) *Love, Guilt and Reparation and Other Works 1921–1945*, London.

Klein, V. (1965) *Britain's Married Women Workers*, Routledge & Kegan Paul, London.

Koshuk, R.P. (1947) Developmental records of 500 nursery school children. In: *Journal of Experimental Education* 16: 134–48.

Kruithof, B. (1982) Continuïteit in opvoedingsadviezen in protestants Nederland van de 17e tot de 19e eeuw. In: *Sociologisch Tijdschrift* 9: 476–92.

Laan, T. van der and W. Tubbergen (1986) *'Zij voelen zich een groep . . . en dat vinden ze fijn!'*, Rijksuniversiteit, Utrecht.

Labov, W. (1972) The logic of nonstandard English. In: *Language and Social Context*, P. Gigliolo (ed.), Harmondsworth.

Lasch, C. (1977) *Haven in a Heartless World: The Family Besieged*, New York.

Lazar, I. (1983) Discussion and implications of the findings. In: *As the twig is bent . . .* The Consortium for Longitudinal Studies, LEA, Hillsdale, NJ.

Lazerson, M. (1972) The historical antecedents of early childhood education. In: *Early Childhood Education: The 71st Yearbook of the National Society for the Study of Education*, Chicago.

Leinster-Mackay, D.P. (1976) Dame schools: a need for review. In: *British Journal of Educational Studies* 24: 33–48.

LeVine, R.A. (1983) A cross-cultural perspective on parenting. In: *Parenting in a Multi-Cultural Society*, M.D. Fantini and R. Cárdenas, New York.

Levine, M. and A. Levine (1970) *A Social History of Helping Services: Clinic, Court, School and Community*, New York.

Levy, D.M. (1966) *Maternal Overprotection*, New York (1943).

Lewis, J. (1980) *The Politics of Motherhood: Child and Maternal Welfare in England, 1900–1939*, London.

Lieberman, A.F. (1978) Psychology and day care. In: *Social Research* 45: 416–51.

Locke, J. (1964) Some thoughts concerning education. In: *John Locke and Education*, P. Gay (ed.) New York (1690).

Lomax, E. The Laura Spelman Rockefeller Memorial: some of its contributions to early research in child development. In: *Journal of the History of the Behavioral Sciences* 13: 283–93.

Lomax, E.M.R. (1978) *Science and Patterns of Child Care*, San Francisco.

McCann, P. and F.A. Young (1982) *Samuel Wilderspin and the Infant School Movement*, London.

McCann, W.P. (1966) Samuel Wilderspin and the early infant schools. In: *British Journal of Educational Studies* 14: 188–204.

Madden, J., O'Hare, J. and P. Levenstein (1984) Home again: effects of the mother–child home program on mother and child. In: *Child Development* 55: 636–47.

Mahler, S.M., Pine, F. and A. Bergman (1980), *Die psychische Geburt des Menschen. Symbiose und Individuation*, Frankfurt am Main.

Mannoni, M. (1977) *Het kind, zijn 'ziekte' en de anderen*, Deventer.

Marks, P. (1976) Femininity in the classroom: an account of changing attitudes. In: *The Rights and Wrongs of Women*, J. Mitchell and A. Oakley (eds), Harmondsworth.

Mayall, B. and P. Petrie (1977) *Minder, Mother and Child*, London.

Miller, A. (1981) *Du sollst nicht merken*, Suhrkamp, Frankfurt am Main.
—— (1983) *In den beginne was er opvoeding*, Bussem.
Miller, L.B. (1979) Development of curriculum models in Head Start. In: *Project Head Start, a Legacy of the War on Poverty*, E. Zigler and J. Valentine (eds), The Free Press, New York.
Moustakas, C.E. (1952) Personality studies conducted in nursery schools. In: *Journal of Educational Research* 44: 161–77.
Mueller, M. (1928) *Frauen im Dienste Fröbels*, Leibzig.
Mulder, H. (1827) *Opmerkingen en wenken voor opvoeders en onderwijzers, betreffende de vroege vorming der jeugd in de daartoe bestemde inrigtingen*, The Hague.
Myrdal, A. and V. Klein (1956) *Women's Two Roles: Home and Work*, London.
Neill, A.S. (1971) *Summerhill*, Harmondsworth (1962).
Newcombe, N. and J.C. Lerner (1982) Britain between the wars: the historical context of Bowlby's theory of attachment. In: *Psychiatry* 45: 1–12.
Newson, J. and E. Newson (1974) Cultural aspects of childrearing in the English-speaking world. In: *The Integration of a Child into a Social World*, M.P.M. Richards (ed.), London.
Nye, I.F. and L.W. Hoffman (1963) *The Employed Mother in America*, Chicago.
O'Connor, N. (1956) The evidence for the permanently disturbing effects of mother child separation. In: *Acta Psychologica* XII: 174–92.
O'Keefe, R.A. (1979) What Head Start means to families. In: *Current Topics in Early Childhood Education*, vol. II, L.G. Katz (ed.), Ablex Publ. Corp. Norwood, NJ.
Owen, J. Dale (1968) The principles of natural education. In: *Utopianism and Education: Robert Owen and the Owenites*, J.F.C. Harrison (ed.), New York.
Owen, R. (1967) *The Life of Robert Owen, Written by Himself, with Selections from his Writings and Correspondence*, vol. I, London (1857).
—— (1968a) The rules for an infant school. In: *Utopianism and Education, Robert Owen and the Owenites*, John F.C. Harrison (ed.), New York.
—— (1968b) The institution for the formation of character. In: *Utopianism and Education, Robert Owen and the Owenites*, John F.C. Harrison (ed.), New York.
—— (1968c) A new view of society (1813–1814). In: *Utopianism and Education, Robert Owen and the Owenites*, J.F.C. Harrison (ed.), New York.
Owen, R. Dale (1968) Education at New Lanark. In: *Utopianism and Education, Robert Owen and the Owenites*, J.F.C. Harrison (ed.), New York.
Palmer, F.H. and L.W. Anderson (1979) Long-term gains from early intervention: findings from longitudinal studies. In: *Project Head Start, a Legacy of the War on Poverty*, E. Zigler and J. Valentine (eds), The Free Press, New York.
Pederson, J.S. (1972) Schoolmistresses and headmistresses: elites and education in 19th century England. In: *Journal of British Studies* 15.
Pence, A.R. (1986) Infant schools in North America, 1825–1840. In: *Adva-*

nces in Early Education and Day Care, vol. 4, S. Kilmer (ed.), Norwood, NJ.

Pestalozzi, J.H. (1804) *Het boek der moeders of handleiding voor moeders en haare kinderen opmerken en spreeken te leeren*, Groningen.

—— (1923) *Hoe Gertrui haar kinderen onderwijst, bewerkt door J.H. Huijts*, Rotterdam (1801).

—— (1956) *Brieven over de opvoeding van het jonge kind, gericht aan J.P. Greaves*, Amsterdam (1818).

Philippi-Siewertsz van Reesema, C. (1949) *Pioniers der Volksopvoeding*, The Hague.

Philipson, I. (1982) Narcissism and mothering: the 1950s reconsidered. In: *Women's Studies International Forum* 5: 29–50.

Phillips, A. and P. Moss (1988) *Who Cares for Europe's Children? The Short Report of the European Childcare Network*, Commission of the European Communities, Brussels.

Phillips, D. (1987) Infants and child care: the new controversy. In: *Child Care Information Exchange*, Nov.: 19–22.

—— (1990) Day care for young children in the United States. In: *Day Care for Young Children, International Perspectives*, E.C. Melhuish and P. Moss (eds), Routledge, London.

Piaget, J. (1933) Children's philosophies. In: *Handbook of Child Psychology*, C. Murchison (ed.), Worcester, Mass.

Pines, M. (1967) *Revolution in Learning*, Harper & Row, New York.

Pinneau, S.R. (1955) The infantile disorders of hospitalism and anaclitic depression. In: *Psychological Bulletin* 52: 429–52.

Platt, A.M. (1977) *The Child Savers, The Invention of Delinquency*, 2nd edition, enlarged, Chicago.

Powell, D.R. (1977) Correlates of parent–teacher communication frequency and diversity. In: *The Journal of Educational Research* 71: 333–41.

—— (1978) The interpersonal relationship between parents and caregivers in day care settings. In: *American Journal of Orthopsychiatry* 48: 680–9.

—— (1980a) Strategies for helping parents find child care: a research perspective. In: *Advances in Early Education and Day Care*, vol. III, S. Kilmer (ed.), Greenwich, Conn.

—— (1980b) Toward a socioecological perspective of relations between parents and child care programs. In: *Advances in Early Education and Day Care*, vol. I, S. Kilmer (ed.), Greenwich.

—— (1984) Enhancing the effectiveness of parent education: an analysis of program assumptions. In: *Current Topics in Early Childhood Education*, vol. V, L.G. Katz (ed.), Norwood, NJ.

Preyer, W. (1882/1985) *Die Seele des Kindes: Beobachtungen uber die geistige Entwicklung des Menschen in den ersten Lebenjahren*, 4th edition, Leipzig.

Preschool and Parental Education (1929) 28th Yearbook of the National Society for the Study of Education, Part I, G.M. Whipple (ed.), Bloomington, Ill.

Prinsen, P.J. (1820) *Pestalozzi's leerwijze in de kennis der getallen*, Leyden.

Provence, S. (1982) Infant day care: relationships between theory and practice. In: *Day Care, Scientific and Social Policy Issues,* E.F. Zigler and E.W. Gordon, Boston.

Ramey, C.T., Dorval, B. and L. Baker-Ward (1983) Group day care and socially disadvantaged families: effects on the child and the family. In: *Advances in Early Education and Day Care,* vol. III, S. Kilmer (ed.), Greenwich, Conn.

Ramey, C.T., Bryant, D.M. and T.M. Suarez (1985) Preschool compensatory education and the modifiability of intelligence: a critical review. In: *Current Topics in Human Intelligence,* vol. I, D.K. Detterman (ed.), Norwood, NJ.

Rappart, I. von (1961) *Die Bedeutung der Mutter bei J.H. Pestalozzi,* Bonn.

Ribble, M. (1965) *The Rights of Infants: Early Psychological Needs and their Satisfaction,* New York (1943).

Ricciuti, H.N. (1974) Fear and the development of social attachments in the first year of life. In: *The Origins of Fear,* M. Lewis and L.A. Rosenblum (eds), New York.

Richards, M. and P. Light (eds) (1986) *Children of Social Words,* Cambridge.

Richmond, J.B., Stipek, D.J. and E. Zigler (1979) A decade of Head Start. In: *Project Head Start, a Legacy of the War on Poverty,* E. Zigler and J. Valentine (eds), The Free Press, New York.

Richters, J.E. and C. Zahn-Waxler (1988) The infant day care controversy: current status and future directions. In: *Early Childhood Research Quarterly* 3: 319–36.

Rijkens, R.G. (1845) *De bewaarschool. Praktische handleiding ten dienste van hen, die bewaarscholen wenschen op te rigten en daarin werkzaam zijn,* Groningen.

Rijswijk-Clerkx, L.E. van (1981) *Moeders, kinderen en kinderopvang,* Nijmegen.

Riley, D. (1983) *War in the nursery: Theories of the Child and Mother,* London.

Roberts, A.F.B. (1972) A new view of the infant school movement. In: *British Journal of Educational Studies* 20: 154–64.

Roby, P. (ed.) (1973) *Child Care, Who Cares?* Foreign and Domestic Infant and Early Childhood Development Policies, New York.

Rose, N. (1979) The psychological complex: mental measurement and social administration. In: *Ideology and Consciousness* 5: 5–68.

Ross, C.L. (1979) Early skirmishes with poverty: the historical roots of Head Start. In: *Project Head Start, a Legacy of the War on Poverty,* E. Zigler and J. Valentine (eds), The Free Press, New York.

Ross, D. (1972) *G. Stanley Hall,* Chicago.

Ross, E. Dale (1976) *The Kindergarten Crusade: the Establishment of Preschool Education in the United States,* Ohio.

Rousseau, J.J. (1983) *Emile of over de opvoeding,* Meppel.

Rubenstein, J. and C. Howes (1983) Social-emotional development of toddlers in day care: the role of peers and of individual differences. In: *Advances in Early Education and Day Care,* vol. III, S. Kilmer (ed.), Greenwich, Conn.

Rubenstein, J.L., Pedersen, F.A. and L.J. Yarrow (1977) What happens when mother is away: a comparison of mothers and substitute care-givers. In: *Developmental Psychology* 13: 529–30.

Rusk, R.R. (1933) *A History of Infant Education*, London.

Rutter, M. (1972) *Maternal Deprivation Reassessed*, Harmondsworth.

—— (1979) Maternal deprivation, 1972–1978: new findings, new concepts, new approaches. In: *Child Development* 50: 283–305.

—— (1981) Social-emotional consequences of day care for preschool children. In: *American Journal of Orthopsychiatry* 51: 4–28.

Sale, J.S. (1979) Implementation of a Head Start Preschool Education Program: Los Angeles, 1965–1967. In: *Project Head Start, a Legacy of the War on Poverty*, E. Zigler and J. Valentine (eds), The Free Press, New York.

Scarr, S. and K. McCartney (1988) Far from home: an experimental evolution of the mother–child home program in Bermuda. In: *Child Development* 59: 531–43.

Schachter, F.F. (1979) *Everyday Mother Talk to Toddlers: Early Intervention*, Academic Press, New York.

Schlossman, S. (1973) Conservative applications of recapitulation theory: G. Stanley Hall and the Boy's Club. In: *Journal of the History of the Behavioral Sciences* 9: 140–7.

—— (1976) Before Home Start: notes toward a history of parent education in America 1897–1929. In: *Harvard Educational Review* 46: 436–67.

—— (1978) The parent education game: the politics of child psychology in the 1970s. In: *Teacher College Record* 79: 788–808.

—— (1981) Philanthropy and the gospel of child development. In: *History of Education Quarterly* 21: 275–99.

Schwartz, P. (1983) Length of day-care attendance and attachment behavior in eighteen-month-old infants. In: *Child Development* 54: 1073–8.

Sears, P.S. and E.M. Dowley (1963) Research on teaching in the nursery school. In: *Handbook of Research on Teaching*, N.L. Gage (ed.), Chicago.

Sears, R. R. (1975) Your ancients revisited: a history of child development. In: *Review of Child Development Research*, vol. 5, E. Mavis Hetherington (ed.), Chicago.

Segal, H. (1974) *Introduction to the Work of Melanie Klein*, New York.

Senn, M.J.E. (1975) Insights on the child development movement in the United States, *Monographs of the Society for Research in Child Development*, serial no. 161., vol. 40, Aug.

Setten, H. van (1982) Opvoedend onderwijs. De vernieuwing van het Nederlandse volksonderwijs in het begin van de vorige eeuw. In: *Comenius* 2: 5–36.

Shapiro, M.S. (1985) *Child's Garden: The Kindergarten Movement from Froebel to Dewey*, The Pennsylvania State University Press, Pennsylvania.

Siegel, A.W. and S.H. White (1982) The child study movement: early growth and development of the symbolized child. In: *Advances in Child Development and Behavior*, vol. 17, H.W. Reese (ed.), New York/London.

Silver, P. and H. Silver (1974) *The Education of the Poor*, 1824–1974, London/Boston.

Silverstein, L. (1981) A critical review of current research on infant day care. In: *Child Care, Family Benefits, and Working Parents*, S.B. Kamerman and A.J. Kahn, New York.

Singer, E. (1989) *Kinderopvang en de moeder–kindrelatie*, Deventer.

Sjølund, A. (1973) *Daycare Institutions and Children's Development*, Westmead, Farnborough, Hants.

Skeels, H.M. (1966) Adult status of children with contrasting early life experiences, *Monographs of the Society for Research in Child Development* 31.

Skeels, H.M. and H.B. Dye (1939) A study of the effects of differential stimulation on mentally retarded children. In: *Proceedings of the American Association on Mental Deficiency* 44: 114–36.

Sluckin, W. (ed.) (1968) *Early Learning and Early Experience*, Harmondsworth.

Smith, G. and T. James (1975) The effects of preschool education: some American and British evidence. In: *Oxford Review of Education* 1: 223–40.

Snyder, A. (1972) *Dauntless Women in Childhood Education: 1856–1931*, Washington, DC.

Spitz, R. (1945) Hospitalism: an inquiry into the genesis of psychiatric conditions in early childhood. In: *The Psychoanalytic Study of the Child* 1: 53–74.

Spodek, B. (1982) The kindergarten: a retrospective and contemporary view. In: *Current Topics in Early Childhood Education*, vol. IV, L.G. Katz (ed.), Ablex, Norwood, NJ.

Sroufe, L.A. (1988) A developmental perspective on day care. In: *Early Childhood Research Quarterly* 3: 283–91.

Stayton, D.J., Hogan, R. and M.D. Salter Ainsworth (1971) Infant obedience and maternal behavior: the origins of socialization reconsidered. In: *Child Development* 42; 1057–69.

Steere, G. (1968) Freudianism and child-rearing in the twenties. In: *American Quarterly* 20: 759–67.

Steinfels, M. O'Brien (1973) *Who's Minding the Children? The History and Politics of Day Care in America*, New York.

Stewart, W.A.C. and W.P. McCann (1967) *The Educational Innovators 1750–1880*, London.

Stoddard, G.D. and B.L. Wellman (1940) Environment and IQ. In: *Yearbook of the National Society for the Study of Education* 39 (Part I): 405–42.

Stone, J. Galambos (1979) General philosophy: preschool education within Head Start. In: *Project Head Start, a Legacy of the War on Poverty*, E. Zigler and J. Valentine (eds), The Free Press, New York.

Strickland, C. (1973–74) Transcendentalist father: the child-rearing practices of Bronson Alcott. In: *History of Childhood Quarterly* 1: 4–51.

Sulman, M.A. (1973) The humanization of the American child: Benjamin Spock as a popularizer of psychoanalytic thought. In: *Journal of the History of the Behavioral Sciences* 9: 258–65.

Sunley, R. (1955) Early nineteenth-century American literature on child rearing. In: *Childhood in Contemporary Cultures*, M. Mead and M. Wolfenstein (eds), Chicago.

Swift, J.W. (1964) Effects of early group experience: the nursery school and day nursery. In: *Review of Child Development Research*, vol. I, M.L. Hoffman and L.W. Hoffman (eds), New York.

Szreter, R. (1964) The origins of full-time compulsory education at five. In: *British Journal of Educational Studies* XIII: 16–28.

Taylor, B. (1983) *Eve and the New Jerusalem: Socialism and Feminism in the Nineteenth Century*, London.

Taylor-Allen, A. (1982) Spiritual motherhood: German feminists and the kindergarten movement, 1848–1911. In: *History of Education Quarterly* 22: 319–39.

Thompson, R.A. (1988) The effects of infant day care through the prism of attachment theory: a critical appraisal. In: *Early Childhood Research Quarterly* 3: 273–82.

Thorndike, E. (1913) *The Psychology of Learning*, New York.

Tizard, B. and M. Hughes (1984) *Young Children Learning: Talking and Thinking at Home and at School*, London.

Tizard, J., Moss, P. and J. Perry (1976) *All our Children: Preschool Services in a Changing Society*, London.

Tulkin, S.R. (1972) An analysis of the concept of cultural deprivation. In: *Developmental Psychology* 6: 326–39.

Turner, D.A. (1970) 1870: The state and the infant school system. In: *British Journal of Education Studies* 18: 151–65.

Turner, P.H. and E. Zigler (1987) *Parents and Day Care: The Search for an Alliance*, Eric Documentation 300 123.

Valentine, J. and E. Stark (1979) The social context of parent involvement. In: *Project Head Start, a Legacy of the War on Poverty*, E. Zigler and J. Valentine (eds), The Free Press, New York.

Vandewalker, N.C. (1908) *The Kindergarten in American Education*, New York.

Vaughn, B., Govers, F.L. and B. Egeland (1980) The relationship between out-of-home care and the quality of infant–mother attachment in an economically disadvantaged population. In: *Child Development* 51: 1203–14.

Verhulst, F.C. (1985) *Mental Health in Dutch Children*, Rotterdam.

—— (1987) *De toekomst van het kind*, Oratie, Erasmus University, Amsterdam.

Verwoerd, R. (1986) Kindbeeld en pedagogiek in de Nederlandse Verlichting. In: *Comenius* 23: 318–41.

Walkerdine, V. (1984) Developmental psychology and the child-centred pedagogy: the insertion of Piaget into early education. In: *Changing the Subject*, J. Henriques, W. Hollway, C. Urwin, C. Venn and V. Walkerdine (eds), London.

Walkerdine, V. and H. Lucey (1989) *Democracy in the Kitchen*, Virago Press, London.

Washburn, R.W. (1944) Re-education in a nursery group: a study in clinical psychology. In: *Monographs of the Society for Research in Child Development 9*.

Watson, J. (1928) *The Psychological Care of the Infant and Child*, New York.

Weber, E. (1969) *The Kindergarten, Its Encounter with Educational Thought in America*, New York.

Welter, B. (1966) The cult of true womanhood, 1820–1860. In: *American Quarterly* 18: 151–74.

Whitbread, N. (1972) *The Evolution of the Nursery-Infant School: A History of Infant and Nursery-infant Education in Britain 1800–1970*, London.

White, S. (1981) Psychology as a moral science. In: *The Child and Other Cultural Inventions*, F.S. Kessel and A.W. Siegel (eds), New York.

Whitebook, M., Howes, C. and D. Phillips (1990) *Who Cares? Child Care Teachers and the Quality of Care in America: Executive Summary National Child Care Staffing Study*.

Wilson, E. (1977) *Women and the Welfare State*, Tavistock Women's Studies, London.

Winnicott, D.W. (1981a) *The Child, the Family, and the Outside World*, Harmondsworth (first published 1964).

—— (1981b) The deprived child and how he can be compensated for loss of family life. (1950) In: *The Family and Individual Development*, D.W. Winnicott, London.

—— (1982) The theory of the parent–infant relationship, (1960) In: *The Maturational Processes and the Facilitating Environment*, D.W. Winnicott, London.

—— (1984) *Deprivation and Delinquency*, London/New York.

Winter, M. de (1986) *Het voorspelbare kind*, Lisse.

Wishy, B. (1968) *The Child and the Republic: The Dawn of Modern American Child Nurture*, Philadelphia.

Wolf, K. (1945) Evacuation of children in war time. In: *Psychoanalytic Study of the Child* 1: 389–404.

Wolfenstein, M. (1951) The emergence of fun morality. In: *The Journal of Social Issues* 7: 15–25.

Wolff, B. (1977) *Proeve over de opvoeding, aan Nederlandsche moeders. Inleiding in versvorm van Agatha Deken*, Meppel (1780).

Wolzogen-Kuehr, S.I. von (1920) *De Nederlandsche vrouw in de tweede helft der 18e eeuw*, Leyden.

Woodham-Smith, P. (1952) History of the Froebel movement in England. In: *Friedrich Froebel and English Education*, E. Lawrence (ed.), London.

Yarrow, L.J. (1961) Maternal Deprivation: toward an empirical and conceptual re-evaluation. In: *Psychological Bulletin* 58: 459–90.

Zigler, E. and K. Anderson (1979) An idea whose time had come: the intellectual and political climate. In: *Project Head Start, a Legacy of the War on Poverty*, E. Zigler and J. Valentine (eds), The Free Press, New York.

Zigler, E.F. and E.W. Gordon (eds) (1982) *Day Care: Scientific and Social Policy Issues*, Boston.

Zigler, E. and J. Valentine (eds) (1979) *Project Head Start, a Legacy of the War on Poverty*, The Free Press, New York.

Name index

Subject index